Spanish
Middle School / High School

By
Cynthia Downs

Cover Design by
Annette Hollister-Papp

Illustrations by
Marty Bucella

Publisher
Carson-Dellosa Publishing, LLC
Greensboro, North Carolina

Credits

Author.. Cynthia Downs
Artist.. Marty Bucella
Cover Design .... Annette Hollister-Papp
Cover Photograph....................................... © 1999 Corbis Corp.
Project Director/Editor.. Kelly Morris Huxmann
Spanish Consultants....................Language for Industry Worldwide, Inc.
and Jessica Orme
Graphic Design and Layout.. Mark Conrad

Visit carsondellosa.com for correlations to Common Core, state, national, and Canadian provincial standards.

09-100171151

ISBN 0-88724-758-X

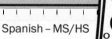

Table of Contents

The Alphabet 4

In the Classroom 5

What Does It Mean? 6

What's Your Name? 7

How Are You? 8

I Would Like to Introduce 9

Introductions 10

Numbers 11–12

Number Practice 13

Battle of the Boats 14

Number Review 15

Ordinal Numbers 16

Days of the Week 17

Months of the Year 18

The Seasons 19

How Is the Weather? 20

Dates 21

Pronouns 22

Practice with Pronouns........................23

The Gender of Nouns 24

Plural Nouns 25

Articles 26

What Is It? 27

Adjectives...28–29

Colors 30–31

Possession 32

The Family Tree 33

There Is 34

Verbs 35

"Ar" Verbs 36–37

"To Be" (estar) 38–39

In the Home 40

Where Is It? 41

Prepositions 42–43

Gerunds...44

What Are You Doing? 45

"To Be" (ser) 46

More Uses of "Ser" 47

"Ser" or "Estar"?................................48

Where Are You From?.........................49

The Community 50–51

"To Wear" (llevar puesto)..............52–53

"To Put On" (ponerse) 54

"To Play" (jugar, tocar) 55

I Play Sports 56

"Er" Verbs 57

"Ir" Verbs 58

Verb Review 59

Using Verbs 60

Negation 61

"To Have" (tener) 62

Other Uses of "Tener" 63–64

"To Have To" (tener que, hay que) 65

Review with "Tener" 66

More . . . Than 67

Less . . . Than 68

As . . . As 69

Comparisons 70–71

"To Want" (querer) 72

What Do You Want to Do? 73

"To Go" (ir) 74

The Present Progressive 75

Yes or No? 76

What? (¿qué?) 77–78

What Time Is It? (¿qué hora es?) 79–80

At What Time? (¿a qué hora?) 81

Who? (¿quién?) 82

Where? (¿dónde?) 83

When? (¿cuándo?) 84

Which? (¿cuál?) 85

How Much? (¿cuánto?) 86

How? and Why? (¿cómo?, ¿por qué?)................87

Review with Questions 88

An Interview 89

I Like 90

I (Don't) Like 91

What Do They Prefer? 92

"To Give" (dar) 93

Other Uses of "Dar" 94

Practice with "Dar" 95

"To Know" (saber, conocer) 96–97

"To Be Able To" (poder)..............98–99

The Infinitive.................................100–101

The Imperative 102–103

Review 104

Review Crossword 105

Vocabulary.....................................106–112

Answer Key.....................................113–128

El alfabeto / The Alphabet

Learn the sounds of the Spanish alphabet.

La letra	Una palabra	El sonido de la letra
Aa	agua	*a* (h<u>o</u>t)
Bb	bebé	*be* (<u>b</u>oat)
Cc *	cepillo or coco	*ce* (<u>s</u>illy) or (<u>c</u>ola)
CHch **	chocolate	*che* (<u>ch</u>ocolate)
Dd	dedo	*de* (<u>d</u>ay)
Ee	elefante	*e* (r<u>a</u>ke)
Ff	fuego	*efe* (<u>f</u>ire)
Gg *	gato or gigante	*ge* (<u>g</u>oat) or (<u>h</u>ill)
Hh	hoja	*hache* (<u>h</u>our)
Ii	isla	*i* (m<u>ea</u>t)
Jj	jirafa	*jota* (<u>h</u>im)
Kk	koala	*ka* (<u>c</u>at)
Ll	limón	*ele* (<u>l</u>emon)
LLll **	llanta	*elle* (<u>y</u>ellow)
Mm	manzana	*eme* (<u>m</u>ap)
Nn	número	*ene* (<u>n</u>ap)
Ññ	ñu	*eñe* (can<u>y</u>on)
Oo	ocho	*oh* (<u>j</u>oke)
Pp	papalote	*pe* (<u>p</u>illow)
Qq	queso	*cu* (<u>c</u>an)
Rr	rama	*ere* (<u>r</u>ose)
rr ***	perro	*erre* (rolled r sound)
Ss	siete	*ese* (<u>s</u>illy)
Tt	tigre	*te* (<u>t</u>iptoe)
Uu	uvas	*u* (ball<u>oo</u>n)
Vv	violín	*ve* (<u>b</u>aby)
Ww	wafle (no native Spanish words)	*doble ve* (<u>w</u>orm)
Xx	xilófono	*equis* (<u>x</u>ylophone)
Yy	yate	*i griega* (<u>y</u>awn)
Zz	zorro	*zeta* (<u>s</u>et)

* The letters **c** and **g** are pronounced differently, depending on the vowel that follows. A **c** followed by **a, o,** or **u** would be pronounced "k." A **c** followed by an **i** or **e** is pronounced like "s." Similarly, a **g** followed by an **a, o,** or **u** would be pronounced like the **g** in "goat." A **g** followed by an **i** or **e** is pronounced like the **h** in "hill."

** The letter combinations **ch** and **ll** are traditionally considered unique letters in the Spanish alphabet.

*** The letter combination **rr** is not always considered a separate letter, but it is a unique sound in Spanish.

En la clase / In the Classroom

Below you will find a list of common classroom objects. Listen to your teacher pronounce the words in Spanish. After you hear each word, repeat the word yourself. Think about Spanish pronunciation rules as you listen to and say each word.

el alfabeto	alphabet
el altavoz	loudspeaker
la bandera	flag
el bolígrafo	pen
el borrador	eraser
la calculadora	calculator
el calendario	calendar
la cartelera	bulletin board
la cinta	tape
la computadora	computer
el crayón	crayon
la grapadora	stapler
la lámpara	lamp
el lápiz	pencil
el libro	book
la luz	light (overhead)
el mapa	map
la mesa	table
el papel	paper
la papelera	wastepaper basket
la pared	wall
el pegamento	glue

el pincel	paintbrush
la pintura	paint
el piso	floor
el pizarrón	chalkboard
la puerta	door
el pupitre	desk
la regla	ruler
el reloj	clock
el sacapuntas	pencil sharpener
la silla	chair
las tijeras	scissors
la tiza	chalk
la ventana	window

el arte	art
la ciencia	science
la educación física	physical education
los estudios sociales	social studies
la historia	history
la lectura	reading
las matemáticas	mathematics
la música	music

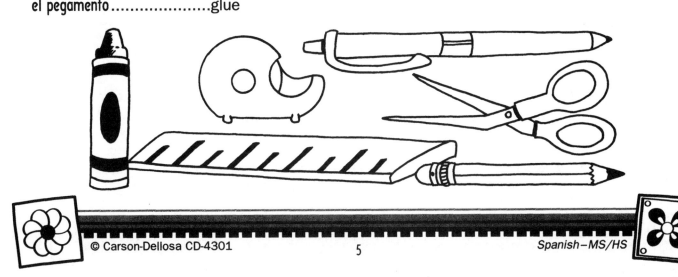

¿Qué quiere decir? / What Does It Mean?

Most Spanish speakers are polite and show respect for each other in their greetings. They usually shake hands when introduced and when they leave, and they will stand to greet you if seated.

¡Hola!...Hello!

¡Buenos días! ....Good morning!

¡Buenas tardes! ....Good afternoon! (This is used until the sun sets.)

¡Buenas noches! ....Good evening or good night!

¡Adiós! ....Good-bye!

¡Hasta luego! ....See you later!

¡Hasta mañana! ....See you tomorrow!

Señor ....Mr.

Señora...Mrs.

Señorita ....Miss or Ms.

don ....title of respect for a man—*don Luis*

doña..title of respect for a woman—*doña Marta*

¿Qué quiere decir...?............................What does . . . mean?

Quiere decir... ....It means . . .

¡Lo siento! ....I am sorry!

¡Perdone!...Excuse me!

Por favor ....Please

¡Gracias!..Thank you!

¡De nada! ....You're welcome!

¡No es nada! ....It's nothing!

¡El gusto es mío!................................The pleasure is mine! or Pleased to meet you!

¡Igualmente!......................................Equally! or Likewise!

* Note: In Spanish, questions and exclamations are "surrounded" by punctuation marks. There is one mark at the beginning of the sentence and another at the end.

¿Cómo te llamas? / What's Your Name?

In Spanish, there is more than one way to ask a person's name. The phrase you choose depends on the situation.

▶ To ask a fellow student or a young child, use the familiar form: ¿Cómo te llamas [tú]?

▶ To ask an adult or a person who commands respect, use the formal form: ¿Cómo se llama [usted]?

▶ To ask more than one person at one time, use the plural form: ¿Cómo se llaman [ustedes]?

▶ To tell someone your own name, use this phrase: Me llamo [your name].

(You will learn more about the distinction between familiar and formal forms as you learn more Spanish.)

Escriba las frases en español.
Write the Spanish phrases.

¿Cómo te llamas? _____ ¿Como te llamas? _____

¿Cómo se llama? _____ ¿Como se llama _____

¿Cómo se llaman? _____ ¿Como se llaman? _____

Me llamo [your name]. _____ Me llamo Ferdinand _____

¿Cuál es la pregunta correcta? Escriba la pregunta en la línea.
What is the correct question? Write the question on the line.

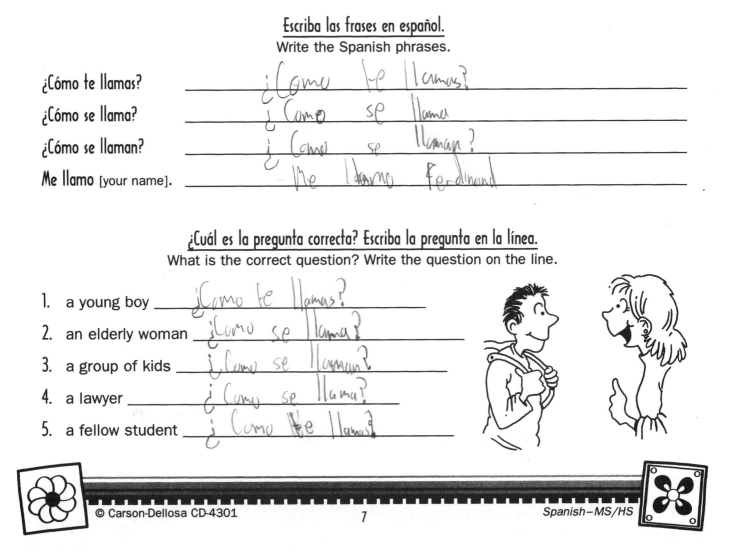

1. a young boy _____ ¿Como te llamas? _____

2. an elderly woman _____ ¿Como se llama? _____

3. a group of kids _____ ¿Como se llaman? _____

4. a lawyer _____ ¿Como se llama? _____

5. a fellow student _____ ¿Como te llamas? _____

¿Cómo estás? / How Are You?

As with "What's your name?" there are several ways to ask, "How are you?" in Spanish.

- To ask how a friend is doing or feeling, say: ¿Cómo estás? or ¿Qué tal?
- In a more formal situation, one would say: ¿Cómo está [usted]?
- To ask more than one person, one could say: ¿Cómo están ustedes?

There are many ways to respond to these questions, too,
including well, so-so, not well, happy, sad, and sleepy.

Escriba la palabra correcta al contestar la pregunta, "¿Cómo estás?"
Write the correct word to answer the question, "How are you?"

1. My dog died. I feel . . . _____triste_____

2. I passed the test. I feel . . . _____feliz_____

3. I could not sleep last night. I feel . . . ___cansado___

4. I have the flu. I feel . . . _____mal_____

5. It's been a great day. I feel . . . _____bien_____

6. I feel neither good nor bad. I feel . . . ___más o menos___

Me gustaría presentar... / I Would Like to Introduce...

Spanish has a formal verb form that is used to address adults or people in a position of respect. **Usted** is the formal form of the word "you." **Ustedes** is the plural form.

The informal verb form is used with children, friends, and family. **Tú** is the informal form of the word "you." **Vosotros** is the plural form of tú, but it is rarely used except in Spain. In Mexico and many other Spanish-speaking countries, **ustedes** is used for the informal plural of "you."

It is important to remember these distinctions in the case of introductions. When in doubt, use the formal form.

▸ A formal introduction:

Me gustaría presentar al Señor Rodríguez.*

¡Buenos días!.........................	Good morning!
¿Cómo está?	How are you?
Muy bien, gracias................	Very well, thank you.
¿Y usted?...........................	And you?

* Note the use of **al** (a + el) before the masculine title **señor**.
Use **a** before a person's name and **a la** before a feminine title
followed by a name. Examples: **a Miguel** or **a la Señora Harris**

▸ An informal introduction:

Me gustaría presentar mi amigo, Darrel.

¡Buenos días!	Good morning!
¿Cómo estás?............................	How are you?
Muy bien, gracias.	Very well, thank you.
¿Y tú?	And you?

Introduce your friends following the examples above.

Example: Hola, Carlita. Me gustaría presentar a _mi amigo, Cristian_.
Shake hands. How should the other person respond?

Once you have practiced informal introductions by introducing your friends,
practice formal introductions by introducing your teacher.

Las presentaciones / Introductions

Escriba las frases en inglés.
Write the phrases in English.

Carla: Mrs. Mendez, I would like to present my friend Jose.

Carla: Sra. Méndez, me gustaría presentar a mi amigo José.

Mrs. Mendez: It's a pleasure to meet you!

Sra. Méndez: ¡El gusto es mío!

José: Me too!

José: ¡Igualmente!

Escriba las frases en español.
Write the phrases in Spanish.

Anna: Buenas tardes, Lupe. ¿Cómo estás?

Anna: Good afternoon, Lupe. How are you?

Lupe: Muy bien, gracias. ¿Y tú?

Lupe: Very well, thank you. And you?

Have everyone in the class choose a Spanish first and last name. Introduce two people to each other. Don't forget to shake hands. Did you use señor, señora, and señorita for different people? Then continue, using the greetings you have learned. Write one of your introductions on the lines below.

_____

_____

_____

_____

Los números / Numbers

▸ In Spanish, the numbers 1–15 have their own unique names. After 15, the numbers have names that are really two numbers linked by a **y** or **i**, which mean "and."

▸ The numbers 16–19 and 21–29 have names which consist of the names of two smaller numbers, joined into one word by **i**.

Examples: 18 = dieciocho or "ten and eight"
23 = veintitrés or "twenty and three"

0	cero	10	diez	20	veinte
1	uno	11	once	21	veintiuno
2	dos	12	doce	22	veintidós
3	tres	13	trece	23	veintitrés
4	cuatro	14	catorce	24	veinticuatro
5	cinco	15	quince	25	veinticinco
6	seis	16	dieciséis	26	veintiséis
7	siete	17	diecisiete	27	veintisiete
8	ocho	18	dieciocho	28	veintiocho
9	nueve	19	diecinueve	29	veintinueve

Escriba los números en español.
Write the numbers in Spanish.

20 _____ veinte
11 _____ once
4 _____ cuatro
8 _____ ocho
1 _____ uno
14 _____ catorce

18 _____ dieciocho
0 _____ cero
5 _____ cinco
10 _____ diez
24 _____ veinticuatro
22 _____ veintidós

Los números / Numbers

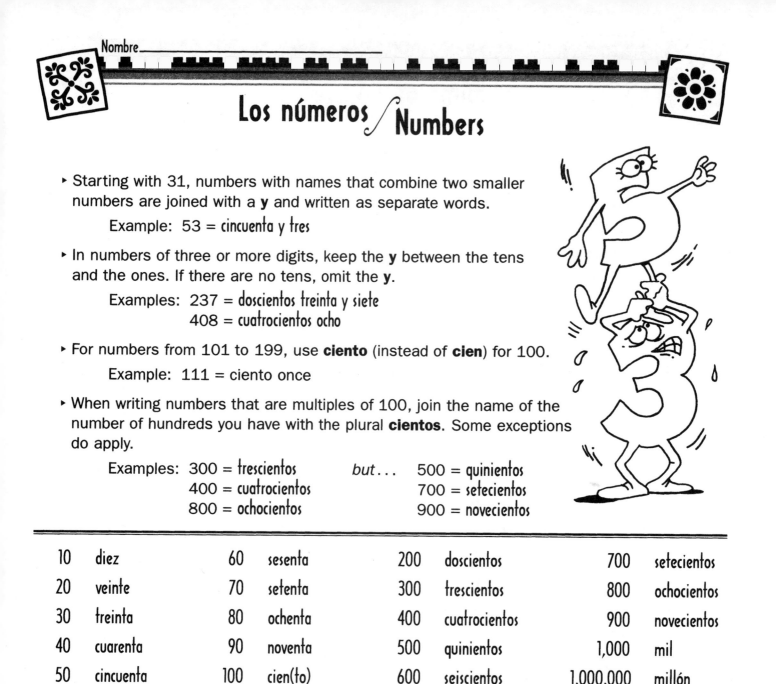

- Starting with 31, numbers with names that combine two smaller numbers are joined with a **y** and written as separate words.

   Example: 53 = cincuenta y tres

- In numbers of three or more digits, keep the **y** between the tens and the ones. If there are no tens, omit the **y**.

   Examples: 237 = doscientos treinta y siete
   408 = cuatrocientos ocho

- For numbers from 101 to 199, use **ciento** (instead of **cien**) for 100.

   Example: 111 = ciento once

- When writing numbers that are multiples of 100, join the name of the number of hundreds you have with the plural **cientos**. Some exceptions do apply.

   Examples: 300 = trescientos   but...   500 = quinientos
   400 = cuatrocientos   700 = setecientos
   800 = ochocientos   900 = novecientos

10	diez	60	sesenta	200	doscientos	700	setecientos
20	veinte	70	setenta	300	trescientos	800	ochocientos
30	treinta	80	ochenta	400	cuatrocientos	900	novecientos
40	cuarenta	90	noventa	500	quinientos	1,000	mil
50	cincuenta	100	cien(to)	600	seiscientos	1,000,000	millón

Escriba los números en español.
Write the numbers in Spanish.

40	cuarenta	1,000	mil
58	cincuenta ocho	212	doscientos doce
120	ciento veinte	704	setecientos cuatro
206	doscientos seis	63	sesenta tres
500	quinientos	99	noventa nueve

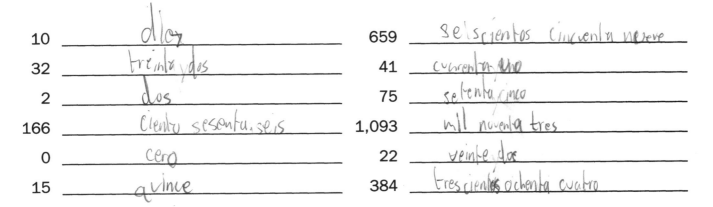

Práctica con números / Number Practice

Escriba los números en español.

10	diez
32	treinta y dos
2	dos
166	ciento sesenta seis
0	cero
15	quince

659	seiscientos cincuenta nueve
41	cuarenta uno
75	setenta cinco
1,093	mil noventa tres
22	veinte dos
384	trescientos ochenta cuatro

Escriba los números.

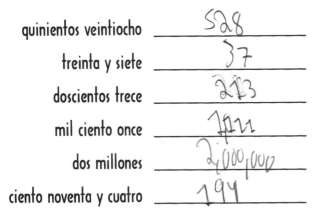

quinientos veintiocho	528
treinta y siete	37
doscientos trece	213
mil ciento once	1111
dos millones	2,000,000
ciento noventa y cuatro	194

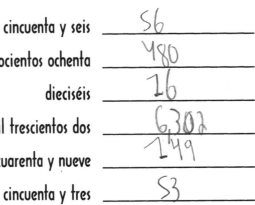

cincuenta y seis	56
cuatrocientos ochenta	480
dieciséis	16
seis mil trescientos dos	6,302
ciento cuarenta y nueve	149
cincuenta y tres	53

Práctica: Número de teléfono
Practice: Telephone Number

Recite your phone number and your best friend's number in Spanish.

‣ First, name the digits in order.
   Example: 555-1234 = "cinco, cinco, cinco, uno, dos, tres, cuatro"

‣ Next, split the phone number into three larger numbers.
   Example: 555-1234 = "quinientos cincuenta y cinco,
                        doce, treinta y cuatro"

Batalla de los barcos / Battle of the Boats

This game is similar to a popular boardgame but is played with barcos, or boats.

Number of Players: 2   **Materials Needed:** 1 copy of this page per player

How to Play:

1. Each player has four boats. Before the game begins, both players fill in spaces on the left-hand grid to show where their boats are located. Boats may only be arranged vertically or horizontally.
2. The first player calls out a number and letter pair from the grid, such as 3-c, asking the opponent, ¿Hay barco en 3c? or "Is there a boat on 3-c?"
3. The opponent responds with sí or no, depending on whether the number called hits one of the boats. The first player records a hit by coloring in the space or a miss by drawing an X on the space in the right-hand grid.
4. When a player hits the last space on a boat, the other player must say ¡Hundido! or "Sunk!"
5. Play continues until one player has sunk all the other's boats. That player wins the game.

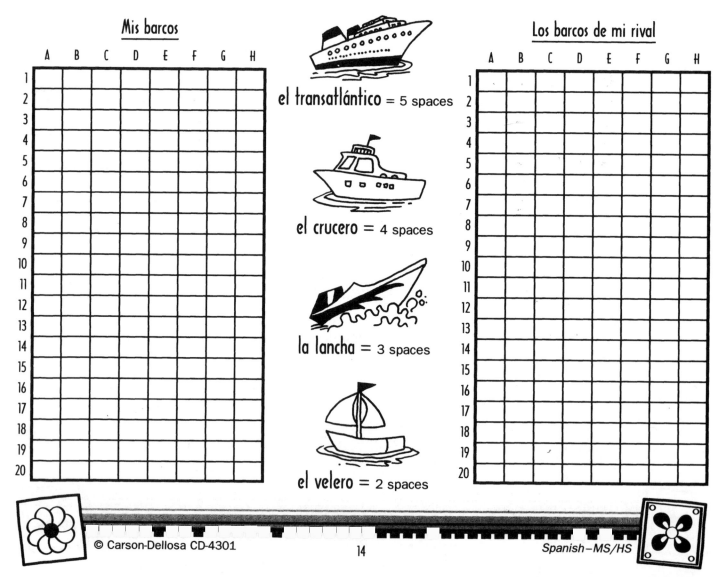

Mis barcos

Los barcos de mi rival

el transatlántico = 5 spaces

el crucero = 4 spaces

la lancha = 3 spaces

el velero = 2 spaces

Repaso de los números / Number Review

Trace una línea entre cada número y las palabras correctas.
Draw a line between each number and the correct number words.

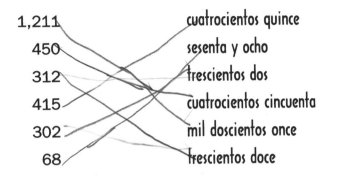

1,211	cuatrocientos quince
450	sesenta y ocho
312	trescientos dos
415	cuatrocientos cincuenta
302	mil doscientos once
68	trescientos doce

Escriba las soluciones en español.
Write the solutions in Spanish.

```
    siete
x   dos
_____
  catorce
```

```
    cinco
-   cinco
_____
   cero
```

```
   veinticinco
x   cuatro
_____
   ciento
```

```
   treinta y uno
+   siete
_____
  treinta ocho
```

```
   cuarenta y uno
-   uno
_____
   cuarenta
```

```
      mil
-  doscientos
_____
  ocho cientos
```

```
    veintinueve
+   uno
_____
   treinta
```

```
    trece
x   tres
_____
  treinta seis
```

```
   ochenta y seis
-   quince
_____
   setenta uno
```

Práctica oral
Oral Practice

‣ Cuente de dos en dos. (Count by twos.)

‣ Cuente de cinco en cinco.

‣ Cuente de diez en diez.

Nombre

Los números ordinales / Ordinal Numbers

Ordinal numbers are numbers that describe position in a sequence. Examples in English include "first" and "third" which are abbreviated as "1st" and "3rd."

In Spanish, ordinal numbers must match the gender of the nouns they modify. Their abbreviations also change to the feminine form (segunda = 2ª) when describing feminine nouns.

1º	primero 1st	first	7º	séptimo..............7th	seventh
2º	segundo..........2nd	second	8º	octavo 8th	eighth
3º	tercero 3rd	third	9º	noveno..............9th	ninth
4º	cuarto 4th	fourth	10º	décimo..............10th	tenth
5º	quinto............5th	fifth	11º	undécimo...........11th	eleventh
6º	sexto 6th	sixth	12º	duodécimo 12th	twelfth

When **primero** or **tercero** is used in front of a masculine noun, the final **o** is dropped.

Examples: **primer libro** (first book), **tercer día** (third day)

Escriba la letra correcta en la línea para contestar la pregunta.
Write the correct letter on the line to answer the question.

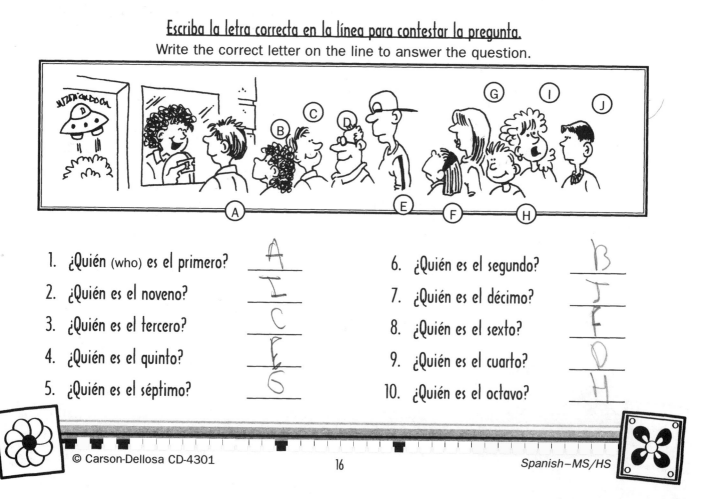

1. ¿Quién (who) es el primero? _A_
2. ¿Quién es el noveno? _I_
3. ¿Quién es el tercero? _C_
4. ¿Quién es el quinto? _E_
5. ¿Quién es el séptimo? _G_

6. ¿Quién es el segundo? _B_
7. ¿Quién es el décimo? _J_
8. ¿Quién es el sexto? _F_
9. ¿Quién es el cuarto? _D_
10. ¿Quién es el octavo? _H_

Los días de la semana / Days of the Week

In Spanish-speaking countries, the week begins with Monday. Days of the week are not capitalized.

Escriba los días de la semana en español.
Write the days of the week in Spanish.

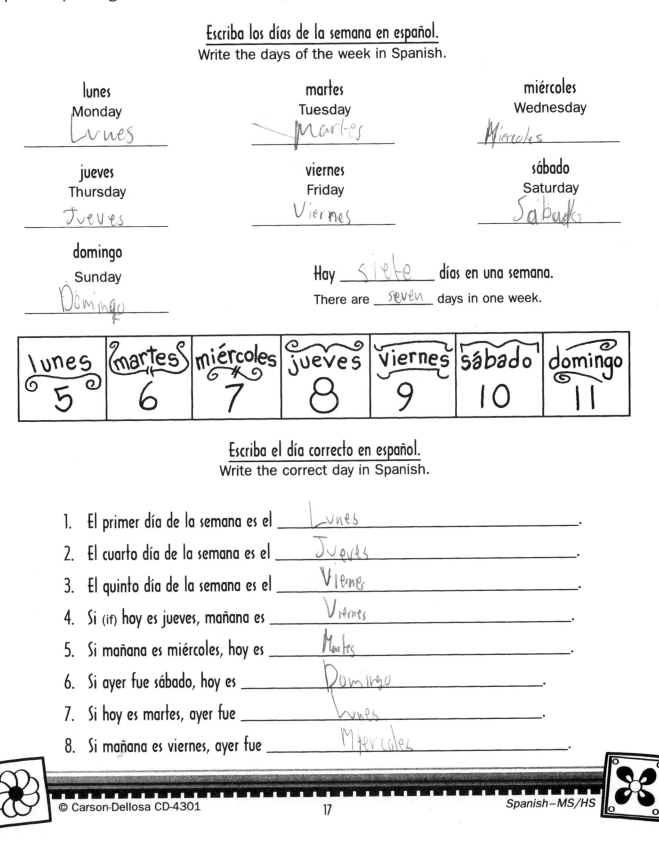

lunes
Monday
Lunes

martes
Tuesday
Martes

miércoles
Wednesday
Miercoles

jueves
Thursday
Jueves

viernes
Friday
Viernes

sábado
Saturday
Sábado

domingo
Sunday
Domingo

Hay ___siete___ días en una semana.
There are ___seven___ days in one week.

lunes	martes	miércoles	jueves	viernes	sábado	domingo
5	6	7	8	9	10	11

Escriba el día correcto en español.
Write the correct day in Spanish.

1. El primer día de la semana es el ___Lunes___.
2. El cuarto día de la semana es el ___Jueves___.
3. El quinto día de la semana es el ___Viernes___.
4. Si (if) hoy es jueves, mañana es ___Viernes___.
5. Si mañana es miércoles, hoy es ___Martes___.
6. Si ayer fue sábado, hoy es ___Domingo___.
7. Si hoy es martes, ayer fue ___Lunes___.
8. Si mañana es viernes, ayer fue ___Miercoles___.

Los meses del año / Months of the Year

Escriba los meses del año en español.
Write the months of the year in Spanish.

enero	Enero	julio	Julio
febrero	Febrero	agosto	Agosto
marzo	Marzo	septiembre	Septiembre
abril	Abril	octubre	Octubre
mayo	Mayo	noviembre	Noviembre
junio	Junio	diciembre	Diciembre

Escriba el mes o el número ordinal correcto para completar cada oración.
Write the correct month or ordinal number to complete each sentence.

1. _____Enero_____ es el primer mes.
2. Diciembre es el _____duodécimo_____ mes.
3. Agosto es el _____Octavo_____ mes.
4. _____Julio_____ es el séptimo mes
5. Abril es el _____Cuatro_____ mes.
6. _____Febrero_____ es el segundo mes.
7. _____Octubre_____ es el décimo mes.
8. _____Marzo_____ es el tercer mes.
9. Mayo es el _____quinto_____ mes.
10. _____Noviembre_____ es el undécimo mes.
11. Junio es el _____Sexto_____ mes.
12. _____Septiembre_____ es el noveno mes.

Las estaciones / The Seasons

Escriba los meses en las líneas.
Write the months on the lines.

el invierno

December, January, February

Diciembre, Enero, Febrero

la primavera

March, April, May

Marzo, Abril, Mayo

el verano

June, July, August

Junio, Julio, Agosto

el otoño

September, October, November

Septiembre, Octubre, Noviembre

¿Qué tiempo hace? / How Is the Weather?

The expressions below describe the weather.

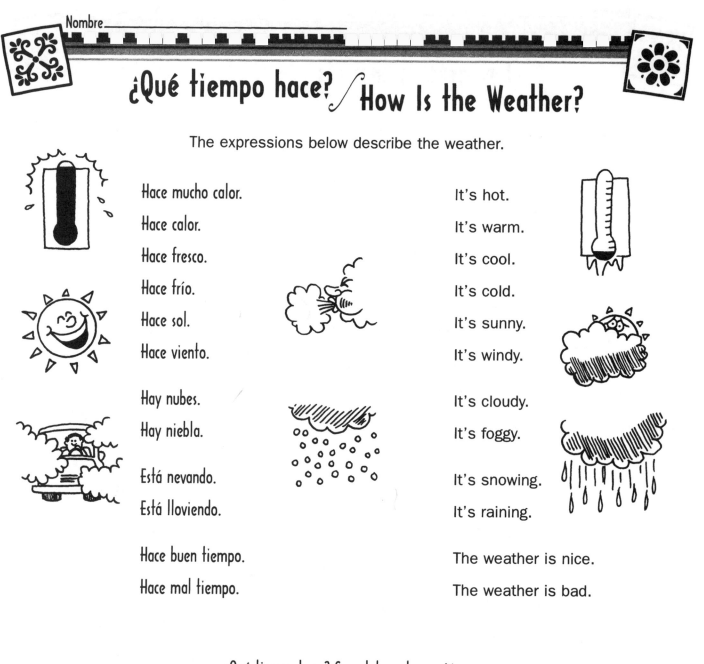

Hace mucho calor.	It's hot.
Hace calor.	It's warm.
Hace fresco.	It's cool.
Hace frío.	It's cold.
Hace sol.	It's sunny.
Hace viento.	It's windy.
Hay nubes.	It's cloudy.
Hay niebla.	It's foggy.
Está nevando.	It's snowing.
Está lloviendo.	It's raining.
Hace buen tiempo.	The weather is nice.
Hace mal tiempo.	The weather is bad.

¿Qué tiempo hace? Complete cada oración.

How is the weather? Complete each sentence.

1. En el invierno _____Hace frío_____.

2. En el verano _____Hace mucho calor_____.

3. En el otoño _____Hace fresco_____.

4. En la primavera _____Hace calor_____.

Las fechas / Dates

In English, dates are given in the order month/day/year.

In Spanish, the month and day are reversed.
Dates are given in the order day/month/year.

Example: March 12, 2002 = 12 de marzo de 2002

Use **primero** for the first day of any month, but use regular numbers after that.

Examples: April 4th = el cuatro de abril
January 1st = el primero de enero

Escriba las fechas en español.
Write the dates in Spanish.

February 3rd — El tercero de Febrero

August 12th — El duodecimo de Agosto

October 2nd — El segundo de Octubre

May 30th — El treinta de Mayo

November 1st — El primero de Noviembre

June 24th — El Veinticuatro de Junio

1. Hoy es ____ el vienticuatro de Marzo ____.

2. Mañana es ____ el vienticinco de Marzo ____.

3. Ayer fue ____ el vientitres de Marzo ____.

4. Mi cumpleaños es ____ el quinto de Mayo ____.

5. El Día de Año Nuevo es ____ el primero de Enero ____.

6. El Día de San Valentín es ____ el catorce de Febrero ____.

7. El primer día de la primavera es ____ el vientiuno de Marzo bre ____.

8. El primer día del otoño es ____ el vientiuno de Septiembre ____.

9. El Día de la Independencia (U.S.) es ____ el cuatro de Julio ____.

10. El Día de la Independencia (Mexico) es ____ el dieciseis de Septiembre ____.

Los pronombres / Pronouns

A **subject pronoun** is a word used to replace the proper name of a subject in a sentence.

Example: Jane is running. — <u>She</u> is running.

"She" is the pronoun used in place of "Jane."

Here are the subject pronouns in Spanish.

Pronombres personales

Singulares		Plurales	
yo I		nosotros/nosotras ....we (masculine/feminine)	
tú ....you (informal)		vosotros/vosotras ....you (plural, informal) *	
usted (Ud.)...........you (formal)		ustedes (Uds.)..............you (plural, informal or formal)	
él ....he/it (masculine)		ellos/ellas...................they (masculine/feminine)	
ella ....she/it (feminine)		* Note that vosotros is used only in Spain.	

As the chart shows, there are many ways to say "you" in Spanish.
To say "you" referring to one person, use tú or usted.
To say "you" referring to more than one person, use vosotros or ustedes.

Escriba el pronombre que usaría para...
Write the pronoun you would use for...

1. "you" when speaking to your sister _____ _yo_

2. "we" when speaking for a girl scout troop _____ _nosotras_

3. yourself _____ _yo_

4. "they" when speaking about your parents _____ _ellos_

5. "you" when speaking to a group of teachers _____ _yo_

6. "you" when speaking to your friends _____ _yo_

Práctica con pronombres / Practice with Pronouns

Escriba el pronombre correcto para cada sujeto.
Write the correct pronoun for each subject.

1. Mr. García   *He*
2. I   *He*
3. Mrs. Nuñez   *She*
4. All of us   *Them*

5. The kids   *Them*
6. You (adult)   *He or she*
7. You (child)   *He or she*
8. We ladies   *Us*

Escriba los plurales.
Write the plurals.

1. yo   *yo*
2. ella   *ella*
3. Ud.   *Ud.*
4. él   *el*
5. tú   *tu*

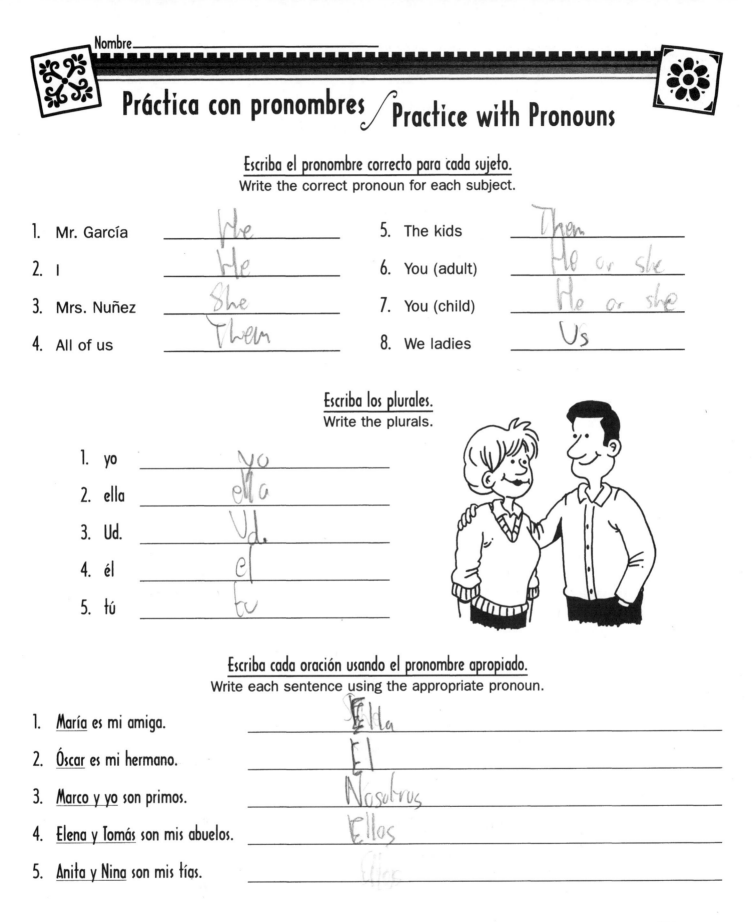

Escriba cada oración usando el pronombre apropiado.
Write each sentence using the appropriate pronoun.

1. María es mi amiga.   *Ella*
2. Óscar es mi hermano.   *El*
3. Marco y yo son primos.   *Nosotros*
4. Elena y Tomás son mis abuelos.   *Ellos*
5. Anita y Nina son mis tías.   *Ellas*

El género de los nombres / The Gender of Nouns

In Spanish, every noun has a **gender**: it is either feminine or masculine. There is no way to know if a word is masculine or feminine simply by knowing what it means. You must learn the gender of each noun along with the word for the noun.

el árbol
(masculine)

la flor
(feminine)

Here are some general rules that apply to the gender of nouns in Spanish.
But be careful—there are always exceptions!

> Most words that end in **a** are feminine. Most words that end in **o** are masculine.

Write **F** next to each feminine noun and **M** next to each masculine noun.

F silla	M dinero	F mesa	F cuchara
F tienda	M plato	M vaso	M perro

* Exceptions to the rule: **día** and **mapa** are masculine, **mano** is feminine.

> Words that end in **ción**, **sión**, **tad**, **dad**, and **umbre** are almost always feminine.

Examples: libertad, conclusión, televisión, lumbre, universidad, nación, personalidad, conversación

> Words that end in **a** but that come from Greek are masculine.

Examples: problema, sistema, idioma, tema, clima, programa, poema, telegrama

Write **F** next to each feminine noun and **M** next to each masculine noun.

M poema	F lumbre	M sistema	M tema
M mapa	M planeta	F fracción	F comunicación
F nación	F universidad	F conversación	F lección

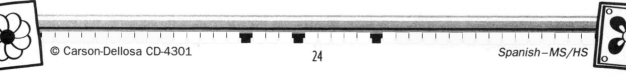

Los nombres plurales / Plural Nouns

It is easy to form the **plural** of a noun in Spanish once you know a few rules.

▸ If the noun ends with a vowel, add **s**.

  Example: el conejo – los conejos

▸ If the noun ends with a consonant, add **es**.

  Example: el árbol – los árboles

▸ If the noun ends with **z**, change it to **c** and add **es**.

  Example: el lápiz – los lápices

▸ If the noun ends with **es** or **is**, it does not change in the plural.

  Example: el lunes – los lunes

Escriba los nombres en plural.
Write the nouns in the plural form.

árbol	Los arboles	flor	Los flores
lombriz	Los lombrices	gato	Los gatos
pájaro	Los pájaros	saltamontes	Los saltamontes
castor	Los castores	pluma	Los plumas
tigre	Los tigres	iguana	Los iguanas
animal	Los animales	planta	Los plantas
hoja	Los hojas	búho	Los búhos
luz	Los luces	conejo	Los conejos
venado	Los venados	ballena	Los ballenas

Artículos / Articles

In Spanish, as in English, there are **definite** and **indefinite** articles.
In Spanish, the article you use depends on the gender of the noun that follows it.

Definite article	**Indefinite article**
(equivalent to English "the")	(equivalent to English "a," "an," or "some")
Use when you are talking about a specific noun or group of nouns.	Use when you are not talking about a specific noun or group of nouns.

el (masculine, singular)
la (feminine, singular)
los (masculine, plural)
las (feminine, plural)

un (masculine, singular)
una (feminine, singular)
unos (masculine, plural)
unas (feminine, plural)

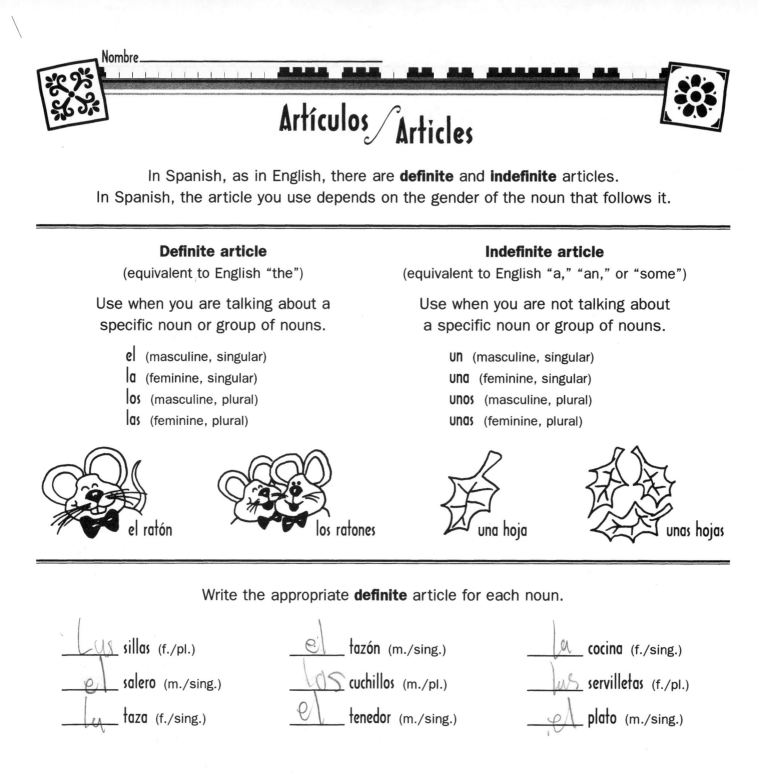

el ratón   los ratones   una hoja   unas hojas

Write the appropriate **definite** article for each noun.

Las sillas (f./pl.)   _el_ tazón (m./sing.)   _la_ cocina (f./sing.)

_el_ salero (m./sing.)   _los_ cuchillos (m./pl.)   _las_ servilletas (f./pl.)

_la_ taza (f./sing.)   _el_ tenedor (m./sing.)   _el_ plato (m./sing.)

Write the appropriate **indefinite** article for each noun.

una comida (f./sing.)   _un_ pimentero (m./sing.)   _un_ comedor (m./sing.)

una mesa (f./sing.)   _un_ vaso (m./sing.)   _un_ mantel (m./sing.)

unas tazas (f./pl.)   _una_ cuchara (f./sing.)   _unos_ platillos (m./pl.)

¿Qué es? / What Is It?

Use ¿Qué es? or ¿Qué son? to ask "What is it?" or "What are they?" in Spanish.
To answer, say Es un/una… or Son unos/unas…

Examples: ¿Qué es?   *Es un mapa.*
           ¿Qué son?   *Son unos crayones.*

Escriba una pregunta y su respuesta apropiada al lado de cada dibujo.
Write one question and an appropriate answer next to each picture.

la bandera — Que es? / Es la bandera

el bolígrafo — Que es? / Es teh bolígrafo

el pegamento — Que es? / Es el pegamento

la ventana — Que es? / Es la ventana

los lápices — Que son? / Son los lápices

el pupitre — Que es? / Es eh pupitre

las sillas — Que son? / Son las sillas

la tiza — Que es? / Es la tiza

la computadora — Que es / Es la computadora

los libros — Que son? / Son los libros

Spanish–MS/HS

Adjetivos / Adjectives

In Spanish, **adjectives** must agree in gender and number with the nouns they modify.

General Rules

▸ Adjectives that end in **o** drop the final **o** and add an **a** after a feminine noun.

    Example: el niño mexicano   la niña mexicana

▸ Adjectives that end in **e** or a consonant do not change after a feminine noun.

    Example: el niño inteligente   la niña inteligente

  Exceptions: Adjectives of nationality that end in a consonant add an **a** in the feminine form.
         Adjectives that end in **án, ón, ín**, or **or** add an **a** to make the feminine form.

    Examples: el hombre inglés   la mujer inglesa
    Examples: el estudiante trabajador   la estudiante trabajadora

▸ Plural adjectives follow the same rules as plural nouns.

    If the adjective ends with a vowel, add **s**.
    If the adjective ends with a consonant, add **es**.
    If the adjective ends with **z**, change it to **c** and add **es**.

▸ When referring to two or more nouns of different genders, always use the masculine form.

    Example: la niña mexicana + el niño mexicano = los niños mexicanos

Cambie los adjetivos siguientes para modificar los sustantivos.
Change the following adjectives to modify the nouns.

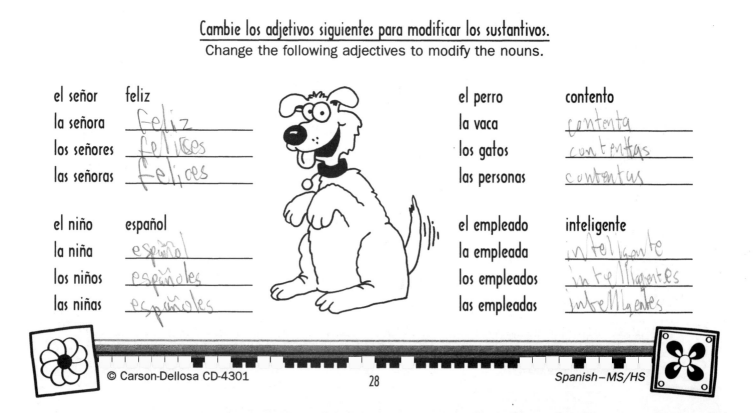

el señor	feliz		el perro	contento
la señora	_feliz_		la vaca	_contenta_
los señores	_felices_		los gatos	_contentas_
las señoras	_felices_		las personas	_contentas_

el niño	español		el empleado	inteligente
la niña	_español_		la empleada	_inteligente_
los niños	_españoles_		los empleados	_inteligentes_
las niñas	_españoles_		las empleadas	_inteligentes_

Adjetivos / Adjectives

In Spanish, most adjectives come after the noun.

    Examples: el gato negro
                  la vaca gigante

Some adjectives that describe number or quantity come *before* the noun.

    Examples: una página
                  muchos libros

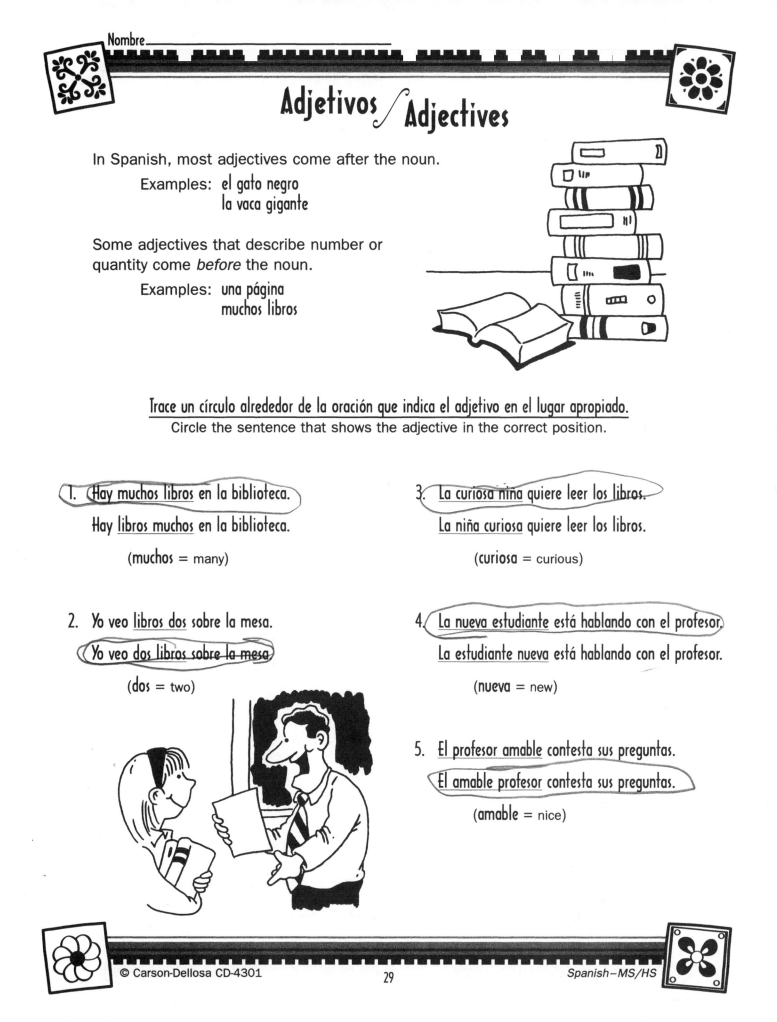

Trace un círculo alrededor de la oración que indica el adjetivo en el lugar apropiado.
Circle the sentence that shows the adjective in the correct position.

1. Hay muchos libros en la biblioteca.

  Hay libros muchos en la biblioteca.

    (muchos = many)

2. Yo veo libros dos sobre la mesa.

  Yo veo dos libros sobre la mesa.

    (dos = two)

3. La curiosa niña quiere leer los libros.

  La niña curiosa quiere leer los libros.

    (curiosa = curious)

4. La nueva estudiante está hablando con el profesor.

  La estudiante nueva está hablando con el profesor.

    (nueva = new)

5. El profesor amable contesta sus preguntas.

  El amable profesor contesta sus preguntas.

    (amable = nice)

Los colores / Colors

Color words are adjectives. When used after a noun,
colors must agree in gender and number with the noun they modify.

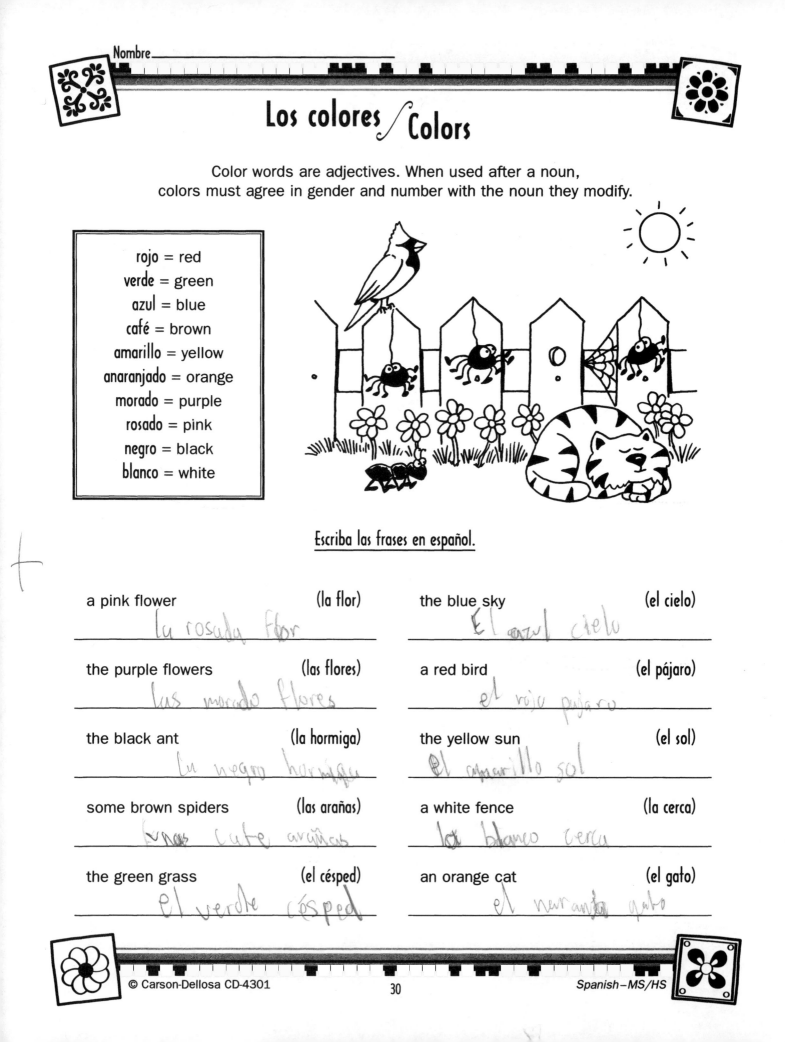

rojo = red
verde = green
azul = blue
café = brown
amarillo = yellow
anaranjado = orange
morado = purple
rosado = pink
negro = black
blanco = white

Escriba las frases en español.

a pink flower   (la flor)

la rosada flor

the purple flowers   (las flores)

las morado flores

the black ant   (la hormiga)

la negro hormiga

some brown spiders   (las arañas)

unas cafe arañas

the green grass   (el césped)

el verde césped

the blue sky   (el cielo)

El azul cielo

a red bird   (el pájaro)

el rojo pájaro

the yellow sun   (el sol)

el amarillo sol

a white fence   (la cerca)

la blanco cerca

an orange cat   (el gato)

el naranja gato

Los colores / Colors

Haga un dibujo de algo...
Draw a picture of something...

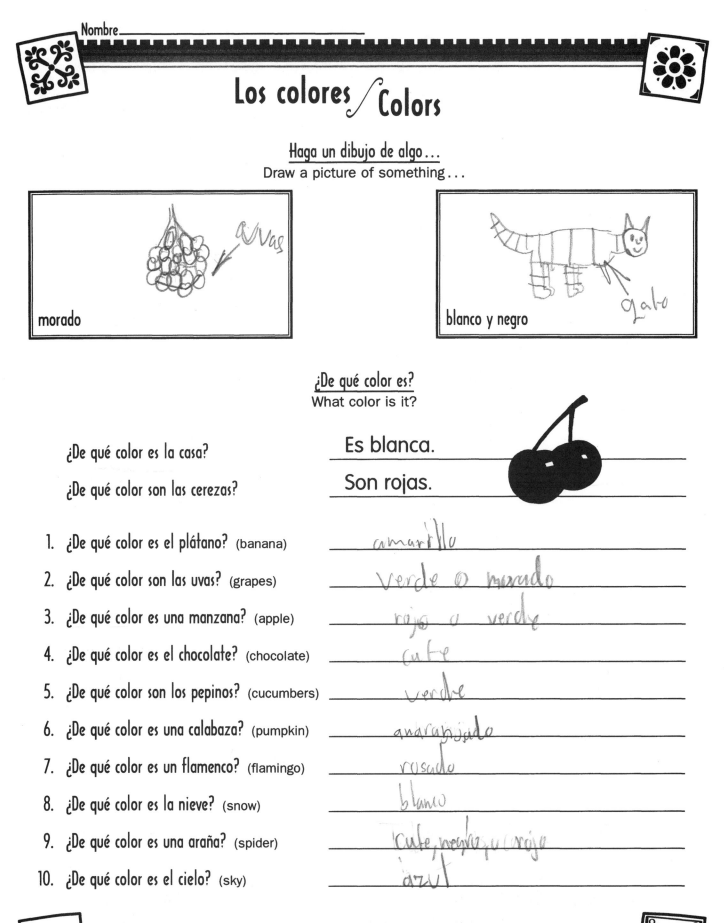

morado

blanco y negro

¿De qué color es?
What color is it?

¿De qué color es la casa?   Es blanca.

¿De qué color son las cerezas?   Son rojas.

1. ¿De qué color es el plátano? (banana)   amarillo

2. ¿De qué color son las uvas? (grapes)   verde o morado

3. ¿De qué color es una manzana? (apple)   roja o verde

4. ¿De qué color es el chocolate? (chocolate)   cafe

5. ¿De qué color son los pepinos? (cucumbers)   verde

6. ¿De qué color es una calabaza? (pumpkin)   anaranjado

7. ¿De qué color es un flamenco? (flamingo)   rosado

8. ¿De qué color es la nieve? (snow)   blanco

9. ¿De qué color es una araña? (spider)   cafe, negra, o roja

10. ¿De qué color es el cielo? (sky)   azul

Nombre_____

La posesión / Possession

There are several ways to show possession in Spanish.
One way is to use **possessive adjectives**, like "my" and "your" in English.

mi	my	nuestro/-a	our
tu	your	vuestro/-a	your (pl.)
su	his/her/its/your (form.)	su	their/your (pl.)

Only nuestro and vuestro change when modifying a feminine noun.
The others remain the same. All of these adjectives add an **s**
when modifying a plural noun.

▸ To describe ownership expressed with "'s" in English,
use the construction [object] + de + [subject].

Examples: my book.................mi libro
John's book ....el libro de John

Escriba las frases en español.

1. our table — nuestro mesa
2. my dog — mi perro
3. their glasses — su lentes
4. your (fam.) pen — su pluma
5. the teacher's ruler — el regla de la maestro
6. Guadalupe's pencil — el lapiz de Guadalupe
7. Luisa's books — los libros de Luisa
8. the boy's chair — el silla de la niño
9. Marc's house — el casa de Marc
10. her plate — su plato

Use the contraction "del" in place of de + el.   Example: la mano del niño

Nombre_____

El árbol genealógico / The Family Tree

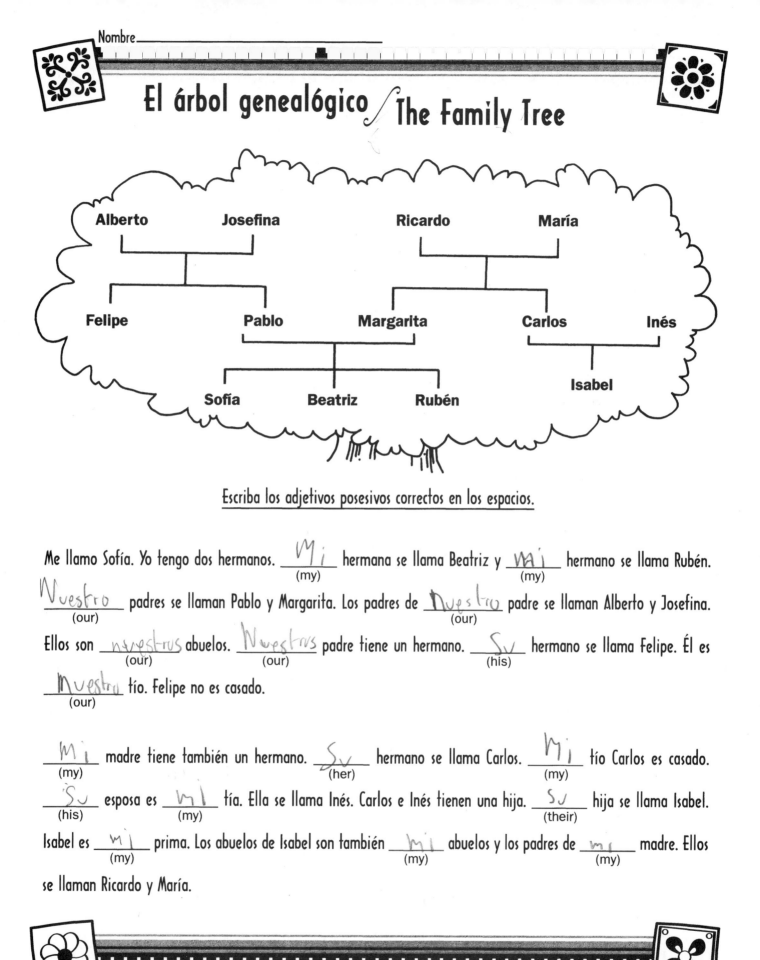

Escriba los adjetivos posesivos correctos en los espacios.

Me llamo Sofía. Yo tengo dos hermanos. __Mi__ (my) hermana se llama Beatriz y __Mi__ (my) hermano se llama Rubén.
__Nuestro__ (our) padres se llaman Pablo y Margarita. Los padres de __Nuestro__ (our) padre se llaman Alberto y Josefina.
Ellos son __nuestros__ (our) abuelos. __Nuestro__ (our) padre tiene un hermano. __Su__ (his) hermano se llama Felipe. Él es
__Nuestro__ (our) tío. Felipe no es casado.

__Mi__ (my) madre tiene también un hermano. __Su__ (her) hermano se llama Carlos. __Mi__ (my) tío Carlos es casado.
__Su__ (his) esposa es __mi__ (my) tía. Ella se llama Inés. Carlos e Inés tienen una hija. __Su__ (their) hija se llama Isabel.
Isabel es __mi__ (my) prima. Los abuelos de Isabel son también __mi__ (my) abuelos y los padres de __mi__ (my) madre. Ellos
se llaman Ricardo y María.

Hay / There Is

The Spanish word hay means "there is" or "there are."

Look at the picture below. Write 10 sentences that describe what you see in the picture.

1. la cómoda	
2. la camisa	
3. el estéreo	
4. la lámpara	
5. el reloj	
6. el ropero	
7. la cama	
8. la merienda	
9. el teléfono	
10. el perro	

¿Qué hay en mi recámara?

What is in my bedroom?

Example: Hay un espejo. (There is a mirror.)

1. Hay la cómoda
2. Hay la camisa
3. Hay el estéreo
4. Hay la lámpara
5. Hay el reloj

6. Hay el ropero
7. Hay la cama
8. Hay la merienda
9. Hay el teléfono
10. Hay el perro

Los verbos / Verbs

The infinitive is a verb in its most complete form. In Spanish, this means a verb with its original ending. Verbs are listed in their infinitive forms in dictionaries and glossaries. The infinitive is also used in many Spanish grammatical structures.

In English, the infinitive includes the word "to."

Examples: to walk, to swim

In Spanish, infinitives generally end in **ar**, **er**, or **ir**.

Examples: hablar, comer, escribir

To **conjugate** a verb means to take its infinitive and break it into the pieces used more frequently when speaking and writing. Follow this formula to change a Spanish verb into a form that is appropriate for a particular subject and verb tense:

> **verb stem** (infinitive – ar, er, or ir) **+ conjugated ending**

This is equivalent to changing "to walk" in English to "she walks."

When you are told to conjugate a verb, it means to find all of the possible forms of that verb in a particular tense. Use the following sequence of subjects when conjugating verbs. When you conjugate, add the stem, or root, of the verb to the ending appropriate for the subject of the sentence and the type of verb (for example, **ar**, **ir**, or **er**).

yo (I)	*hablo*	nosotros/nosotras (we)	*hablamos*
tú (you–singular, informal)	*hablas*	vosotros/vosotras (you–plural, informal)	*habláis*
él/ella/Ud. (he/she/you–singular, formal)	*habla*	ellos/ellas/Uds. (they/they/you–plural, formal)	*hablan*

Write the stem of each verb.

caminar (to work)   *camin*   describir (to describe)   *destrib*

leer (to read)   *le*   saltar (to jump)   *salt*

salir (to leave)   *sal*   vender (to sell)   *vend*

bailar (to dance)   *bail*   cocinar (to cook)   *cocin*

Verbos en "ar" / "Ar" Verbs

All regular **ar** verbs have the same endings when conjugated.
Follow the steps below to conjugate these verbs.

▸ Take off the **ar** ending from the infinitive.
▸ Add one of the endings as shown in the chart.
  Be sure it agrees with the subject of the sentence.

hablar (to speak or talk)

yo	habl<u>o</u>	nosotros/-as	habl<u>amos</u>
tú	habl<u>as</u>	vosotros/-as	habl<u>áis</u>
él/ella/Ud.	habl<u>a</u>	ellos/ellas/Uds.	habl<u>an</u>

Escriba las formas correctas de los verbos.
Write the correct forms of the verbs.

nadar (to swim)

él ___nada___   tú ___nadas___

yo ___nado___   nosotros ___nadamos___

ustedes ___nadan___   ellas ___nadan___

ellos ___nadan___   usted ___nada___

cantar (to sing)

ellos ___cantan___   usted ___canta___

tú ___cantas___   él ___canta___

yo ___canto___   nosotras ___cantamos___

ustedes ___cantan___   ella ___canta___

Verbos en "ar" / "Ar" Verbs

Escriba las formas correctas de los verbos.

mirar (to watch or look at)

yo	miro	nosotros/-as	miramos
tú	miras	vosotros/-as	miráis
él/ella/Ud.	mira	ellos/ellas/Uds.	miran

caminar (to walk)

yo	camino	nosotros/-as	caminamos
tú	caminas	vosotros/-as	camináis
él/ella/Ud.	camina	ellos/ellas/Uds.	caminan

Otros verbos para aprender:
Other verbs to learn:

escuchar to listen	viajar to travel	pintar to paint	completar to complete
terminar to end	enviar to send	llorar to cry	comprar to buy
preguntar to ask	estudiar to study	visitar to visit	encontrar to find

Escriba las frases en español.

we sing ___nosotros cantamos___

I buy ___yo compro___

you (pl.) visit ___Usted visita___

she cries ___ella llora___

we send ___nosotros enviamos___

you introduce ___tu introduces___

they swim ___ellos/-as nadan___

I paint ___yo pinto___

they listen ___ellos/-as escuch___

you (formal) travel ___ella viaja___

Estar / "To Be"

One of the most common verbs you will use in Spanish is estar, which means "to be."
It is an irregular verb, which means that it does not conjugate according to the rules.

estar (to be)

yo	estoy	nosotros/-as	estamos
tú	estás	vosotros/-as	estáis
él/ella/Ud.	está	ellos/ellas/Uds.	están

Refer to this example when you need to decide what each part of a verb means:

yo estoy = I am
tú estás = you (sing.) are
él/ella está = he/she/it is
usted está = you (formal) are

nosotros estamos = we are
vosotros estáis = you (pl., informal) are
ellos/ellas están = they are
ustedes están = you (pl., pl./formal) are

Escriba las oraciones en español.

1. I am happy. _Yo estoy feliz._

2. She is nervous. _Ella esta nervioso._

3. We are sad. _Nosotros estamos triste._

4. You (formal, sing.) are serious. _Usted esta serio._

5. You (sing.) are scared. _Tú estás asustado._

6. They (fem.) are tired. _Usted esta cansado._

7. You (pl.) are angry. _Ustedes estan enojado._

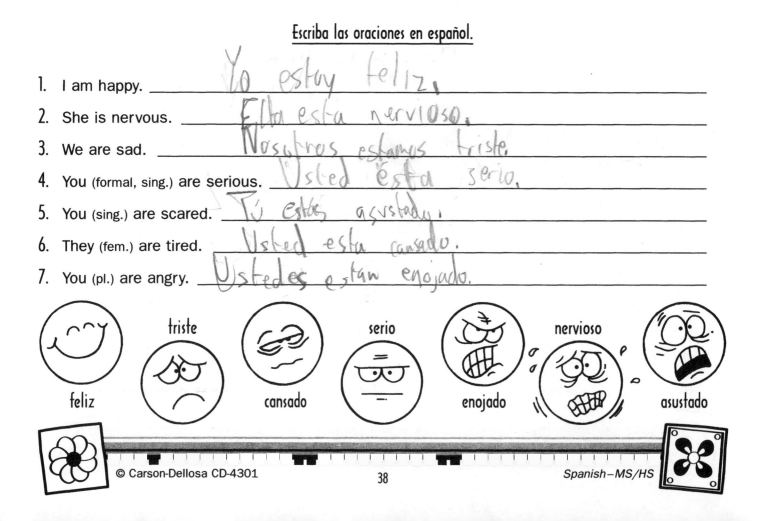

feliz   triste   cansado   serio   enojado   nervioso   asustado

Estar / "To Be"

In Spanish, there are two different verbs that mean "to be."
Both **estar** and **ser** mean "to be," but they are used in different ways.

Some basic uses of **estar**:

▸ To express location

Estoy en casa. = I am at home.

▸ To express a temporary state

Ustedes están enfermos. = You are sick.

▸ To ask and answer questions of "where?"

¿Dónde están los niños? = Where are the boys?
Los niños están en la cafetería. = The boys are in the cafeteria.

Escriba las oraciones en español.

1. My mother is in the kitchen. _Mi mam es en la cocina._

2. We are in the living room. _Nosotros estamos en la sala._

3. Our books are on the table. _Mi libros son encima de la mesa._

4. I am sick today. _Yo soy enfermo hoy._

5. You (sing.) are sick as well. _Tu es enfermo tambien._

6. My brother is bored. _Mi hermano es aburrido._

---

as well (also) = **también**	on the table = **encima de la mesa**
bored = **aburrido**	in the kitchen = **en la cocina**
in the living room = **en la sala**	sick = **enfermo**

Nombre

En la casa / In the Home

Describa los objetos que hay en cada cuarto de la casa.
Describe the objects that are in each room of the house.

Example: En el garaje hay un carro, unas herramientas y una segadora.

En la cocina _estan los gabinetes, la estufa, y el refrigerador._

| el refrigerador | la estufa | los gabinetes |

En el comedor _estan las sillas, la mesa, y el mantel._

| las sillas | la mesa | el mantel |

En la recámara _esta la cama, la comoda, y el ropero._

| la cama | la cómoda | el ropero |

En la sala _estan el sofa, la lámpara, y la alfombra._

| el sofá | la alfombra | la lámpara |

En el baño _estan la ducha, la bañera, y el lavamanos._

| la bañera | la ducha | el lavamanos |

¿Dónde está? / Where Is It?

Conteste las preguntas en español.
Answer the questions in Spanish.

Example: ¿Dónde está la lámpara?
Está en la sala.

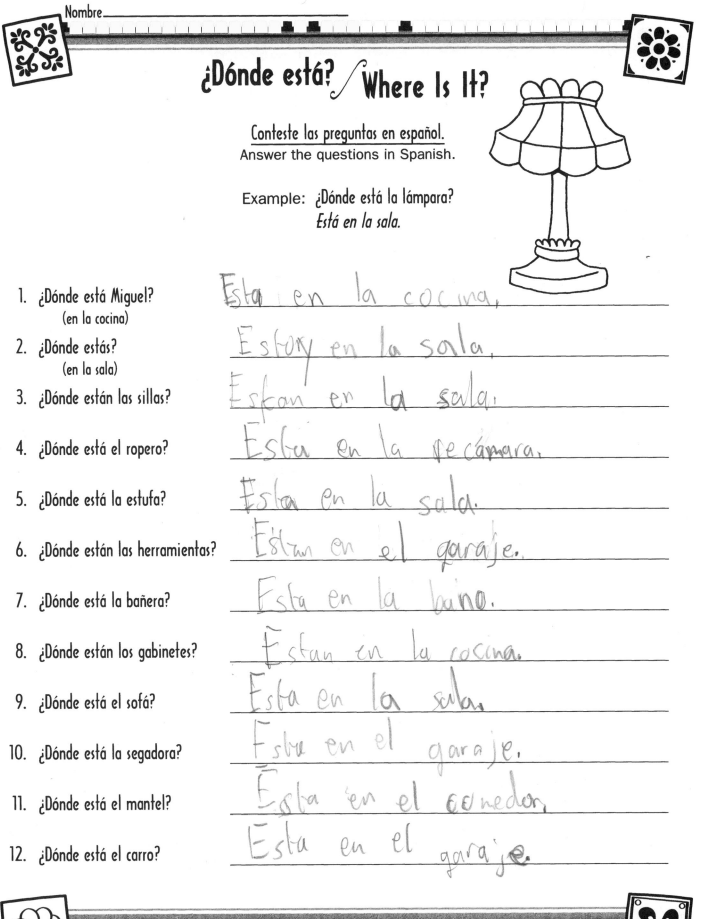

1. ¿Dónde está Miguel?
   (en la cocina)
   Esta en la cocina.

2. ¿Dónde estás?
   (en la sala)
   Estoy en la sala.

3. ¿Dónde están las sillas?
   Estan en la sala.

4. ¿Dónde está el ropero?
   Esta en la recámara.

5. ¿Dónde está la estufa?
   Esta en la sala.

6. ¿Dónde están las herramientas?
   Estan en el garaje.

7. ¿Dónde está la bañera?
   Esta en la bano.

8. ¿Dónde están los gabinetes?
   Estan en la cocina.

9. ¿Dónde está el sofá?
   Esta en la sala.

10. ¿Dónde está la segadora?
    Esta en el garaje.

11. ¿Dónde está el mantel?
    Esta en el comedor.

12. ¿Dónde está el carro?
    Esta en el garaje.

Las preposiciones / Prepositions

Prepositions are words used to help describe location or position.

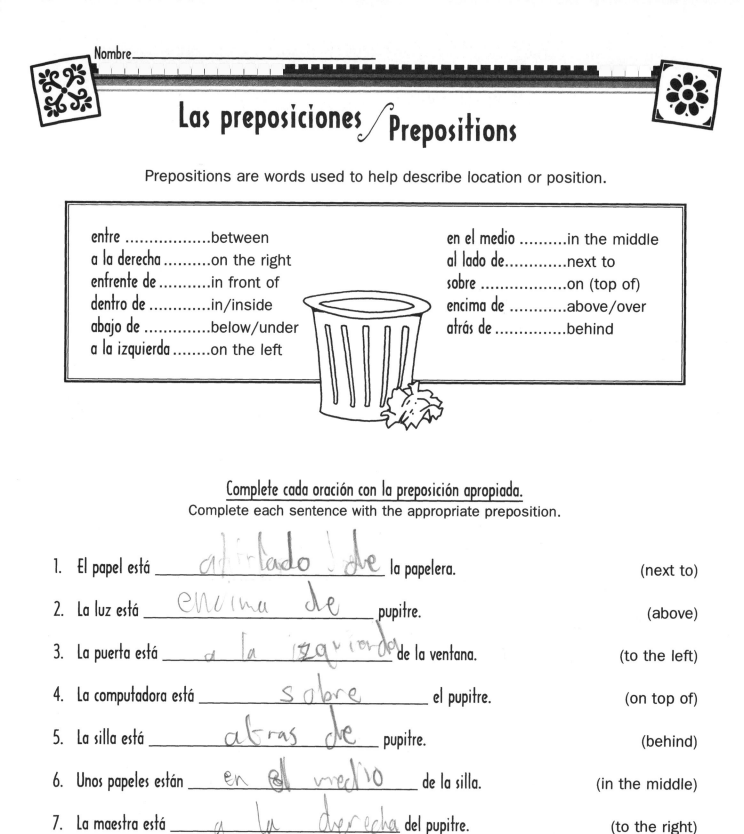

entre ....between		en el medio ....in the middle
a la derecha ....on the right		al lado de.............next to
enfrente de ....in front of		sobre ....on (top of)
dentro de ....in/inside		encima de ....above/over
abajo de ....below/under		atrás de ....behind
a la izquierda ....on the left		

Complete cada oración con la preposición apropiada.
Complete each sentence with the appropriate preposition.

1. El papel está ___al lado de___ la papelera. (next to)

2. La luz está ___encima de___ pupitre. (above)

3. La puerta está ___a la izquierda___ de la ventana. (to the left)

4. La computadora está ___sobre___ el pupitre. (on top of)

5. La silla está ___atras de___ pupitre. (behind)

6. Unos papeles están ___en el medio___ de la silla. (in the middle)

7. La maestra está ___a la derecha___ del pupitre. (to the right)

8. Los estudiantes están ___enfrente de___ la maestra. (in front of)

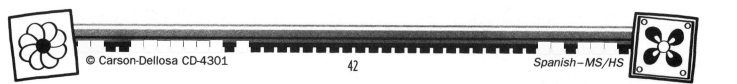

Las preposiciones / Prepositions

Pregunte dónde está cada objeto. Escriba una respuesta para cada pregunta.
Write a question to ask where each object is. Write one answer to each question.

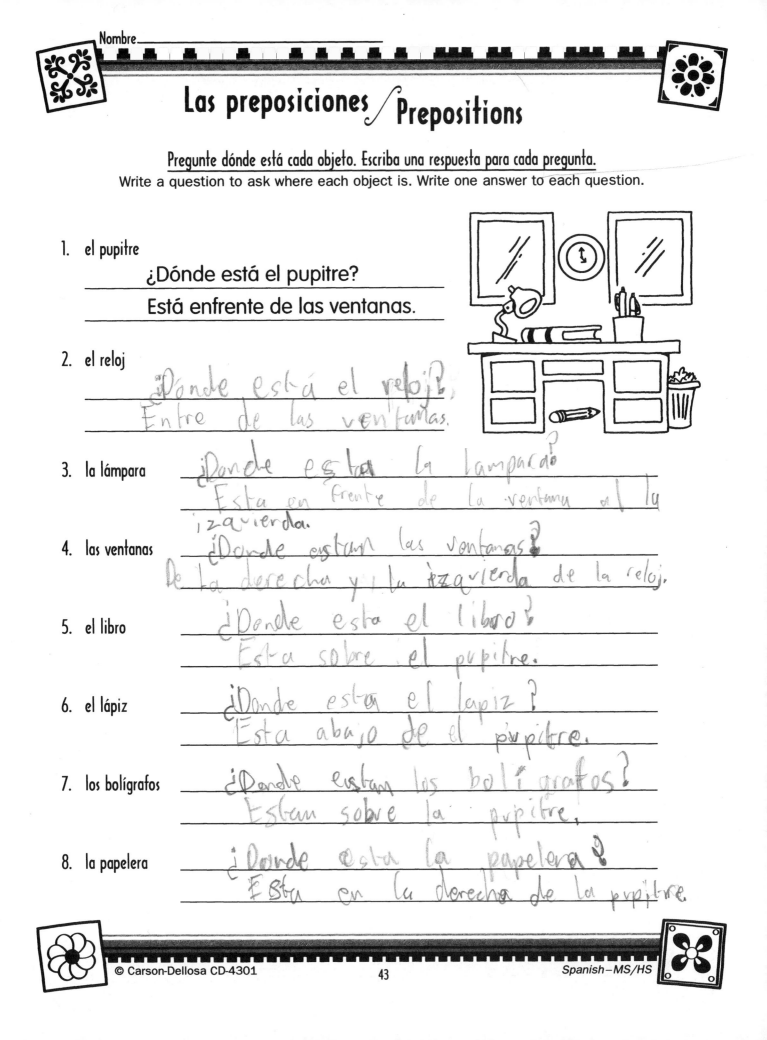

1. el pupitre

    ¿Dónde está el pupitre?

    Está enfrente de las ventanas.

2. el reloj

    ¿Donde está el reloj?

    Entre de las ventanas.

3. la lámpara

    ¿Donde esta la lampara?

    Esta en frente de la ventana a la izqvierda.

4. las ventanas

    ¿Donde estan las ventanas?

    De la derecha y la izqvierda de la reloj.

5. el libro

    ¿Donde esta el libro?

    Esta sobre el pupitre.

6. el lápiz

    ¿Donde esta el lapiz?

    Esta abajo de el pupitre.

7. los bolígrafos

    ¿Donde estan los boligrafos?

    Estan sobre la pupitre.

8. la papelera

    ¿Donde esta la papelera?

    Esta en la derecha de la pupitre.

Los gerundios / Gerunds

When the verb **estar** is used with a gerund ("ing" form of a verb),
it translates as "is doing" or "is making."

Examples: Estoy corriendo. ....I am running.
Él está comiendo. ....He is eating.
Ellas están durmiendo. ....They are sleeping.

To form the gerund:

▸ Verbs that end in **ar** drop the **ar** and add **ando**.

▸ Verbs that end in **er** or **ir** drop the ending
and add **iendo**.

Examples: caminar – ar + ando = caminando
aprender – er + iendo = aprendiendo

Escriba el gerundio de cada verbo.
Write the gerund form of each verb.

caminar _____caminando_____

(to walk)

partir _____partiendo_____

(to leave)

beber _____bebiendo_____

(to drink)

tomar _____tomand____

(to take)

hablar _____hablando_____

(to talk)

escuchar _____eschuchando_____

(to listen to)

escribir _____escribiendo_____

(to write)

saltar _____saltando_____

(to jump)

comer _____comiendo_____

(to eat)

nadar _____nadando_____

(to swim)

bailar _____bailando_____

(to dance)

vivir _____viviendo_____

(to live)

¿Qué haces? / What Are You Doing?

Escriba oraciones completas usando los gerundios.

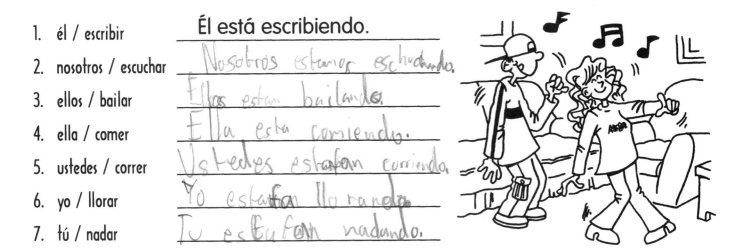

1. él / escribir — **Él está escribiendo.**
2. nosotros / escuchar — Nosotros estamos escuchando.
3. ellos / bailar — Ellos están bailando.
4. ella / comer — Ella esta comiendo.
5. ustedes / correr — Ustedes estaban corriendo.
6. yo / llorar — Yo estaban llorando.
7. tú / nadar — Tu estaban nadando.

Escriba las oraciones en español.

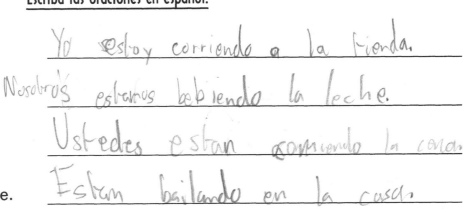

1. I am running to the store.
   (a la tienda) — Yo estoy corriendo a la tienda.
2. We are drinking milk.
   (la leche) — Nosotros estamos bebiendo la leche.
3. You are all eating dinner.
   (la cena) — Ustedes estan comiendo la cena
4. They are dancing in the house.
   (en la casa) — Estan bailando en la casa.

Escriba las oraciones en inglés.

1. Ellos están jugando al fútbol. — They were playing soccer.
2. Estamos escuchando a la maestra. — We're listening to the teacher
3. Estoy hablando con mi amiga. — I'm talking with my friend.
4. Estás llorando. — You're crying.

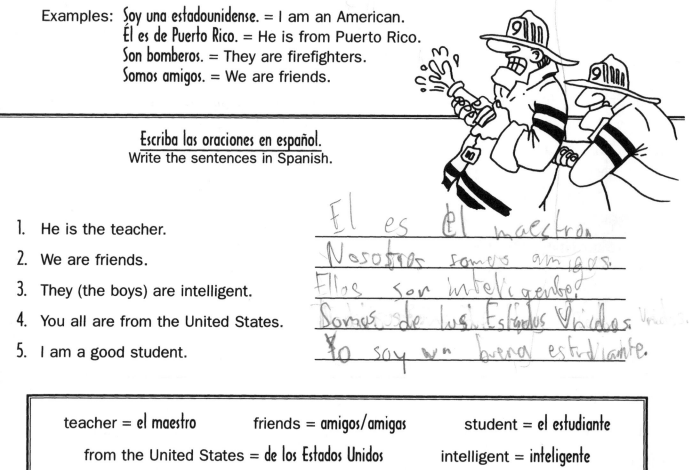

Ser / "To Be"

Ser is another Spanish verb that means "to be."
Like estar, it is an irregular verb and does not conjugate according to the rules.
Unlike estar, ser is used to describe a subject's identity or nature.

ser (to be)

yo	soy	nosotros/-as	somos
tú	eres	vosotros/-as	sois
él/ella/Ud.	es	ellos/ellas/Uds.	son

The most common use of ser is to define the subject or express the subject's basic traits. It is used to describe nationality, profession, relationships (friend, father), and personality traits.

Examples: Soy una estadounidense. = I am an American.
Él es de Puerto Rico. = He is from Puerto Rico.
Son bomberos. = They are firefighters.
Somos amigos. = We are friends.

Escriba las oraciones en español.
Write the sentences in Spanish.

1. He is the teacher.

2. We are friends.

3. They (the boys) are intelligent.

4. You all are from the United States.

5. I am a good student.

Handwritten answers:
1. El es el maestro
2. Nosotros somos amigos.
3. Ellos son inteligentes
4. Somos de los Estados Unidos.
5. Yo soy un buen estudiante.

teacher = el maestro   friends = amigos/amigas   student = el estudiante

from the United States = de los Estados Unidos   intelligent = inteligente

Más usos de "ser" / More Uses of "Ser"

Ser is used to describe a subject's personal characteristics,
including age, character, and appearance.

Examples: Eres vieja. ....You are an old woman.
Ella es amable. ....She is nice.
Él es guapo.......................He is handsome.

Escriba las oraciones en español.

1. We are young. (joven) Nosotros son joven.

2. He is kind. (simpático) El es simpático.

3. The monster is ugly. (el monstruo / feo) El monstruo es feo.

4. The girl is pretty. (la niña / bonita) La niña es bonita.

Ser is also used to express nationality, religion, shape, size, color, and number.

Examples: Ella es de Paraguay. ....She is from Paraguay.
Él es católico. ....He is Catholic.
El árbol es verde. ....The tree is green.
Somos seis. ....We are six. (There are six of us.)

Escriba las oraciones en español.

1. She is from Mexico. Ella es de Mexico.

2. The boy is tall. El niño es alto.

3. She is Hindu. Ella es Hindú.

4. His shirt is green. Su camisa es verde.

from	=	de
tall	=	alto
Hindu	=	hindú
shirt	=	camisa

¿Ser o estar? / "Ser" or "Estar"?

Ser is used in impersonal expressions such as "it is true" or "it is possible," in which "it" does not refer to a particular subject.

Examples: Es verdad que... ....It's true that...
Es posible que... ....It's possible that...

Ser is also used to tell time.

Examples: Es la una. ....It is one o'clock.
Son las dos. ....It is two o'clock.

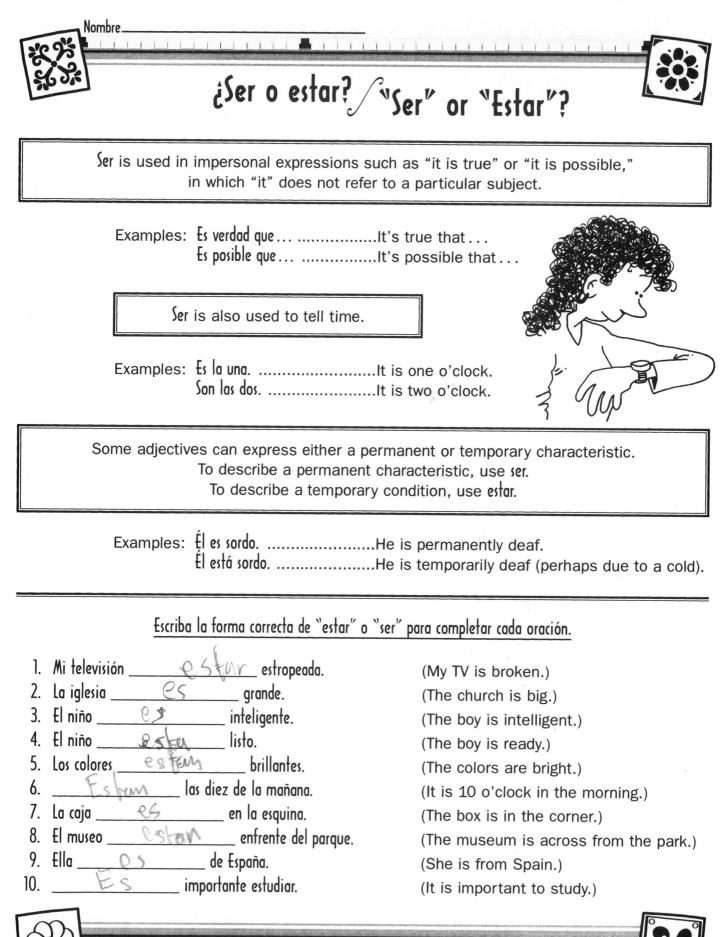

Some adjectives can express either a permanent or temporary characteristic.
To describe a permanent characteristic, use ser.
To describe a temporary condition, use estar.

Examples: Él es sordo. ....He is permanently deaf.
Él está sordo. ....He is temporarily deaf (perhaps due to a cold).

Escriba la forma correcta de "estar" o "ser" para completar cada oración.

1. Mi televisión _____estar_____ estropeada. (My TV is broken.)
2. La iglesia _____es_____ grande. (The church is big.)
3. El niño _____es_____ inteligente. (The boy is intelligent.)
4. El niño _____esta_____ listo. (The boy is ready.)
5. Los colores _____estan_____ brillantes. (The colors are bright.)
6. _____Estan_____ las diez de la mañana. (It is 10 o'clock in the morning.)
7. La caja _____es_____ en la esquina. (The box is in the corner.)
8. El museo _____estan_____ enfrente del parque. (The museum is across from the park.)
9. Ella _____es_____ de España. (She is from Spain.)
10. _____Es_____ importante estudiar. (It is important to study.)

¿De dónde eres? / Where Are You From?

To say that you are from a particular country (or city),
use ser + de + [the country's name].

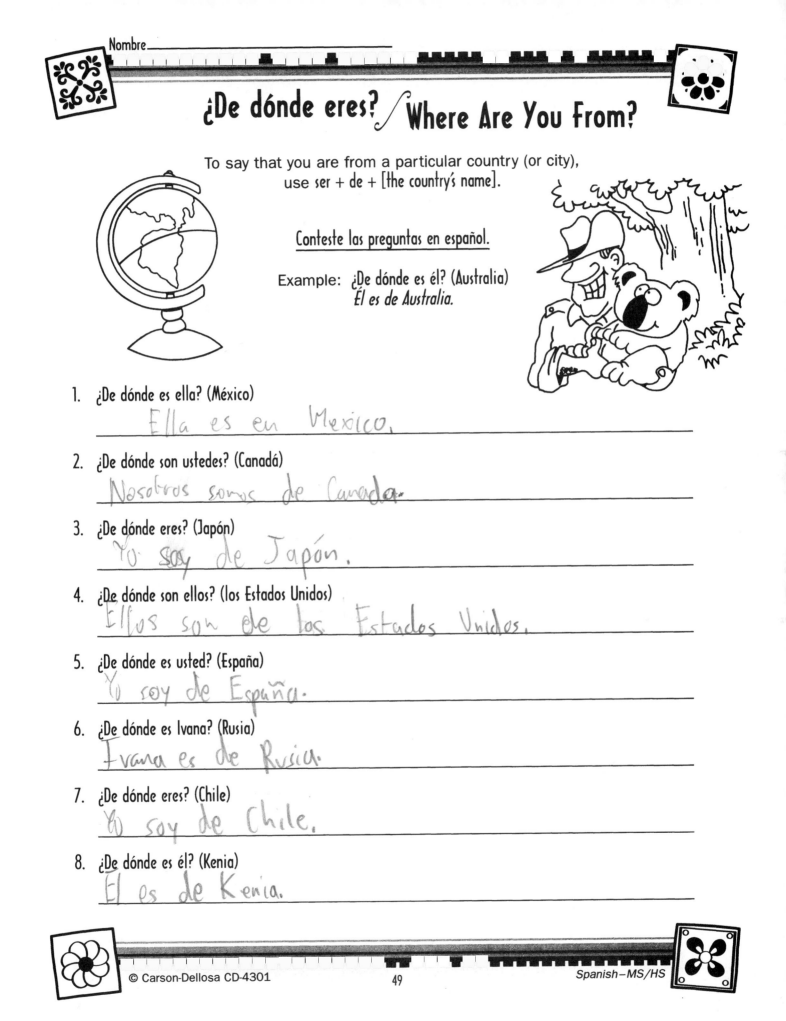

Conteste las preguntas en español.

Example: ¿De dónde es él? (Australia)
Él es de Australia.

1. ¿De dónde es ella? (México)

   Ella es en México.

2. ¿De dónde son ustedes? (Canadá)

   Nosotros somos de Canada.

3. ¿De dónde eres? (Japón)

   Yo soy de Japón.

4. ¿De dónde son ellos? (los Estados Unidos)

   Ellos son de los Estados Unidos.

5. ¿De dónde es usted? (España)

   Yo soy de España.

6. ¿De dónde es Ivana? (Rusia)

   Ivana es de Rusia.

7. ¿De dónde eres? (Chile)

   Yo soy de Chile.

8. ¿De dónde es él? (Kenia)

   Él es de Kenia.

La comunidad / The Community

Trace una línea entre las palabras en español y las palabras en inglés.
Draw a line between the Spanish words and the English words.

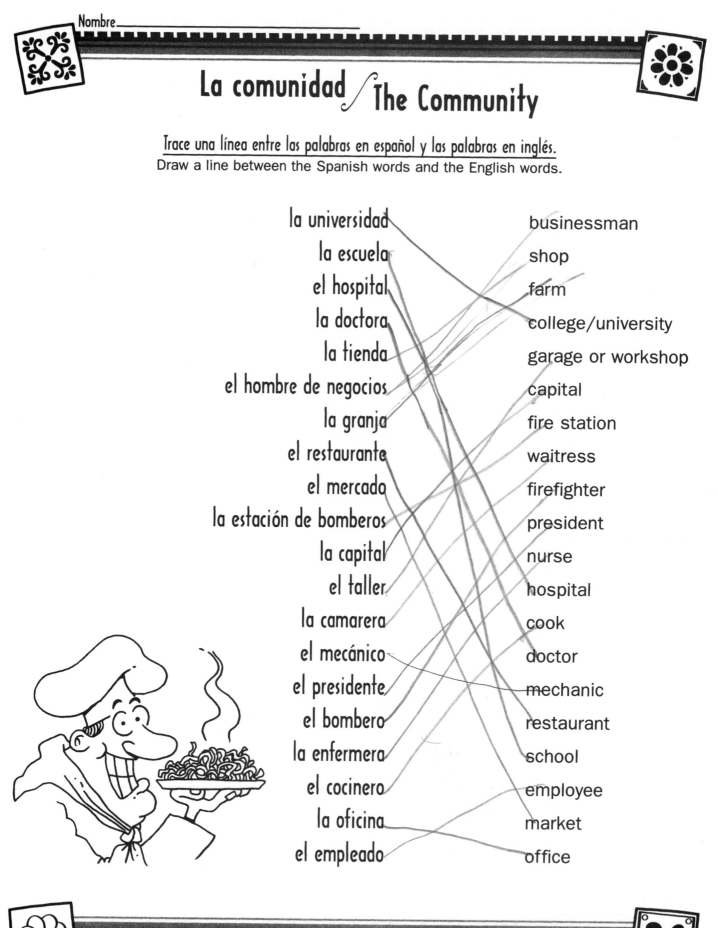

la universidad	businessman
la escuela	shop
el hospital	farm
la doctora	college/university
la tienda	garage or workshop
el hombre de negocios	capital
la granja	fire station
el restaurante	waitress
el mercado	firefighter
la estación de bomberos	president
la capital	nurse
el taller	hospital
la camarera	cook
el mecánico	doctor
el presidente	mechanic
el bombero	restaurant
la enfermera	school
el cocinero	employee
la oficina	market
el empleado	office

La comunidad / The Community

Escriba las formas correctas de "trabajar" y "ser" para completar las oraciones.
Write the correct forms of "to work" and "to be" to complete the sentences.

1. Yo ___trabaja___ en la granja.
   ___ser___ un granjero.

2. Nosotros ___trabajamos___ en el hospital.
   ___seramos___ doctores y enfermeros.

3. Tú ___trabajas___ en el taller.
   ___sera___ una mecánica.

4. Ellos ___trabajan___ en el restaurante.
   Ellos ___seran___ cocineros y camareros.

5. Ella ___trabaja___ en la escuela.
   Ella ___sera___ una maestra.

6. Ustedes ___trabajan___ en la estación de bomberos. Ustedes ___seran___ bomberos.

7. Él ___trabaja___ en la oficina.
   Él ___sera___ un hombre de negocios.

8. Tú ___trabajas___ en la tienda.
   ___sera___ una empleada.

9. Usted ___trabaja___ en la universidad.
   Usted ___sera___ un profesor.

10. Yo ___trabaja___ en la Casa Blanca.
    ___sera___ el presidente.

Trace líneas entre los empleados y sus lugares de trabajo.
Draw lines between the employees and the places they work.

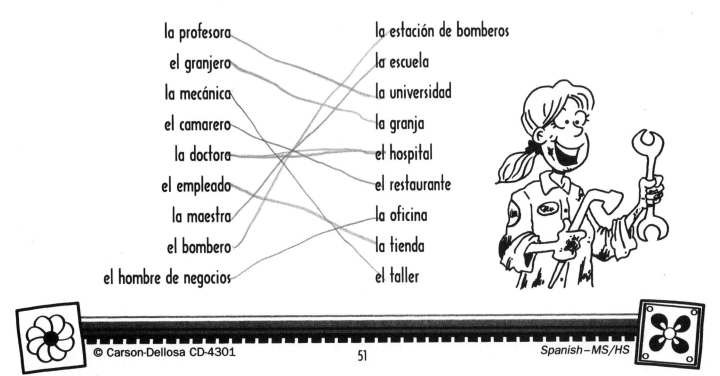

la profesora	la estación de bomberos
el granjero	la escuela
la mecánica	la universidad
el camarero	la granja
la doctora	el hospital
el empleado	el restaurante
la maestra	la oficina
el bombero	la tienda
el hombre de negocios	el taller

Llevar puesto / "To Wear"

When used with articles of clothing, the phrase llevar puesto/a means "to wear."
The adjective puesto must agree in number and gender with the article of clothing.

llevar (to wear)

yo	llevo	nosotros/-as	llevamos
tú	llevas	vosotros/-as	lleváis
él/ella/Ud.	lleva	ellos/ellas/Uds.	llevan

¿Qué llevan puesto las personas? Escriba oraciones completas para describir quién lleva puesta cada cosa.
What are the people wearing? Write complete sentences to describe who wears each thing.

1. yo / la camisa   Llevo puesta una camisa.

2. ella / la blusa   Lleva puesta la blusa.

3. tú / el suéter   Llevas puesta el suéter.

4. usted / los pantalones   Lleva puesta los pantalones.

5. la niña / la falda   Lleva puesta la falda.

6. la mujer / el vestido   Lleva puesta el vestido.

7. nosotros / los calcetines   Llevamos puesta los calcetines.

8. ellas / los zapatos   Lleva puesta los zapatos.

Llevar puesto / "To Wear"

¿Qué llevan puesto las personas? Escriba oraciones completas para describir quién lleva puesta cada cosa.
What are the people wearing? Write complete sentences to describe who wears each thing.

1. tú / los shorts Llevas puesta los shorts.

2. ella / la camiseta Lleva puesta la camiseta.

3. yo / la chaqueta Llevo puesta la chaqueta.

4. usted / el chaleco Lleva puesta el chaleco.

5. el niño / la corbata Lleva puesta la corbata.

6. el hombre / el pijama Lleva puesta el pijama.

7. nosotros / el traje Llevamos puesta el traje.

8. ella / el traje de baño Lleva puesta el traje de baño.

Encuentre y trace un círculo alrededor de las palabras en la sopa de letras.
Find and circle the words in the word search puzzle.

```
Z A P A T O S L I V G E R F L A K C F A Ñ
K N U I U C F J D K I A T A B R O C U I A
P T R A J E D E B A Ñ O Y L S T R O H S S
E F K O A A S U V E S T I D O F O Ñ I A U
B S I Ñ O L M V I D A X M A I S G M V H L
A W T E Y H C A S E N O L A T N A P K O B
E J A R T D E B N J C H A L E C O J U T E
```

falda	camisa
pijama	blusa
traje de baño	corbata
pantalones	chaleco
traje	zapatos
shorts	vestido

Ponerse "To Put On"

Besides wearing clothes, one can also put on clothes.
Use the verb **ponerse** to express this idea.

ponerse (to put on/to wear)

me pongo	I put on	nos ponemos	we put on
te pones	you put on	os ponéis	you (pl.) put on
se pone	he/she/you (form.) put on	se ponen	they/you (pl.) put on

Complete las oraciones.

1. El hombre de negocios se _____pone_____ un traje y una corbata.

2. En el verano los niños se _____pone_____ shorts y camisetas.

3. ¿Te _____pones_____ tu chaqueta? Hoy hace frío.

4. La camarera se _____pone_____ una falda y una blusa.

5. En el invierno nos _____ponemos_____ suéteres, pantalones y calcetines.

6. Cuando voy a la playa, me _____pongo_____ mi traje de baño.

7. Te _____pones_____ tu pijama antes de irte a la cama.

8. Mi hermano se _____pone_____ jeans y una camiseta.

Nombre_____

Jugar y tocar / "To Play"

Jugar and tocar are both verbs that mean "to play." Jugar (an irregular verb) is used with sports and other games, while tocar is used with instruments and types of music.

jugar (to play a game or sport)

yo	juego	nosotros/-as	jugamos
tú	juegas	vosotros/-as	jugáis
él/ella/Ud.	juega	ellos/ellas/Uds.	juegan

Escriba la forma correcta de "jugar" para completar las oraciones.

1. Él _____juega_____ al béisbol.
2. Yo _____juego_____ al fútbol.
3. Nosotras _____jugamos_____ al tenis.
4. ¿Tú _____juegas_____ al golf?
5. Ellas _____juegan_____ al voleibol.

Él es atleta.
Juega a los deportes.

tocar (to play an instrument or music)

yo	toco	nosotros/-as	tocamos
tú	tocas	vosotros/-as	tocáis
él/ella/Ud.	toca	ellos/ellas/Uds.	tocan

Ella es música.
Toca los
instrumentos.

Escriba la forma correcta de "tocar" para completar las oraciones.

1. Ella _____toca_____ el piano.
2. Yo _____toco_____ el tambor.
3. Usted _____toca_____ la trompeta.
4. Nosotros _____tocamos_____ la guitarra.
5. Ustedes _____tocan_____ el violín.

Juego a los deportes / I Play Sports

Lea el párrafo sobre los deportes en los Estados Unidos.
Read the paragraph about sports in the United States.

En los Estados Unidos jugamos a muchos deportes profesionales. En las escuelas, jugamos entre clases diferentes y escuelas diferentes. Cada niño puede competir sólo o en un equipo. Depende del deporte. También, las mujeres pueden jugar en su própio equipo o, algunas veces, pueden jugar con los hombres. El fútbol es un deporte muy popular en México y en los Estados Unidos pero son deportes diferentes. En México, fútbol es lo mismo que "soccer" y fútbol en los Estados Unidos se llama "fútbol americano".

¿Verdadero o falso? Lea cada oración. Escriba "verdadero" o "falso" en la línea.
True or false? Read each statement. Write "true" or "false" on the line.

1. Hay deportes diferentes en los Estados Unidos. _Verdadero_
2. Las mujeres no pueden jugar deportes. _falso_
3. El fútbol en México es diferente del fútbol en los Estados Unidos. _Verdadero_
4. El fútbol es un deporte no muy popular entre los aficionados. _falso_
5. Una persona puede jugar en un equipo o sólo. _Verdadero_
6. Las escuelas juegan a deportes entre sus clases u otras escuelas. _Verdadero_
7. Hay también deportes profesionales en los Estados Unidos. _Verdadero_

Escriba "sí" o "no" para contestar las preguntas.
Write "yes" or "no" to answer the questions.

1. ¿Hay deportes en su escuela? _Sí_
2. ¿Hay equipos con niños y niñas juntos? _No_
3. ¿Juega usted un deporte? _Sí_

Verbos de "er" / "Er" Verbs

You have already learned to conjugate regular verbs that end in **ar**.
Verbs that end in **er** follow the pattern shown in the chart below.

leer (to read)

yo	le<u>o</u>	nosotros/-as	le<u>emos</u>
tú	le<u>es</u>	vosotros/-as	le<u>éis</u>
él/ella/Ud.	le<u>e</u>	ellos/ellas/Uds.	le<u>en</u>

Escriba las formas correctas de los verbos.

	comer (to eat)	vender (to sell)	creer (to believe)
yo	como	vendo	creo
tú	comes	vendes	crees
él/ella	come	vende	cree
Ud.	come	vende	cree
nosotros(as)	comemos	vendemos	creemos
ellos/ellas	comen	venden	creen
Uds.	comen	venden	creen

For more practice, try to conjugate
these verbs out loud: **aprender** (to learn), **beber** (to drink),
correr (to run), and **deber** (to owe).

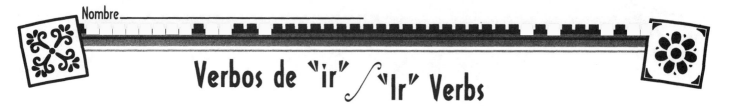

Verbos de "ir" / "Ir" Verbs

Regular verbs that end in **ir** follow nearly the same pattern as verbs that end in **er**.
Only the nosotros and vosotros forms are different.

abrir (to open)

yo	abr<u>o</u>	nosotros/as	abr<u>imos</u>
tú	abr<u>es</u>	vosotros/as	abr<u>ís</u>
él/ella/Ud.	abr<u>e</u>	ellos/ellas/Uds.	abr<u>en</u>

Escriba las formas correctas de los verbos.

	vivir (to live)	escribir (to write)	decidir (to decide)
yo	vivo	escribo	decido
tú	vives	escribes	decides
él/ella	vive	escribe	decide
Ud.	vive	escribe	decide
nosotros(as)	vivimos	escribimos	decidimos
ellos/ellas	viven	escriben	deciden
Uds.	viven	escriben	deciden

Escriba las frases en español.

I open	yo abro	we live	nosotros vivimos
he writes	él escribe	they open	ellos abren
you (pl.) decide	Ustedes deciden	you write	tú escribes

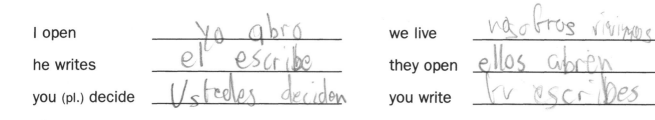

Repaso de los verbos / Verb Review

Escriba los verbos correctos en las cajas.

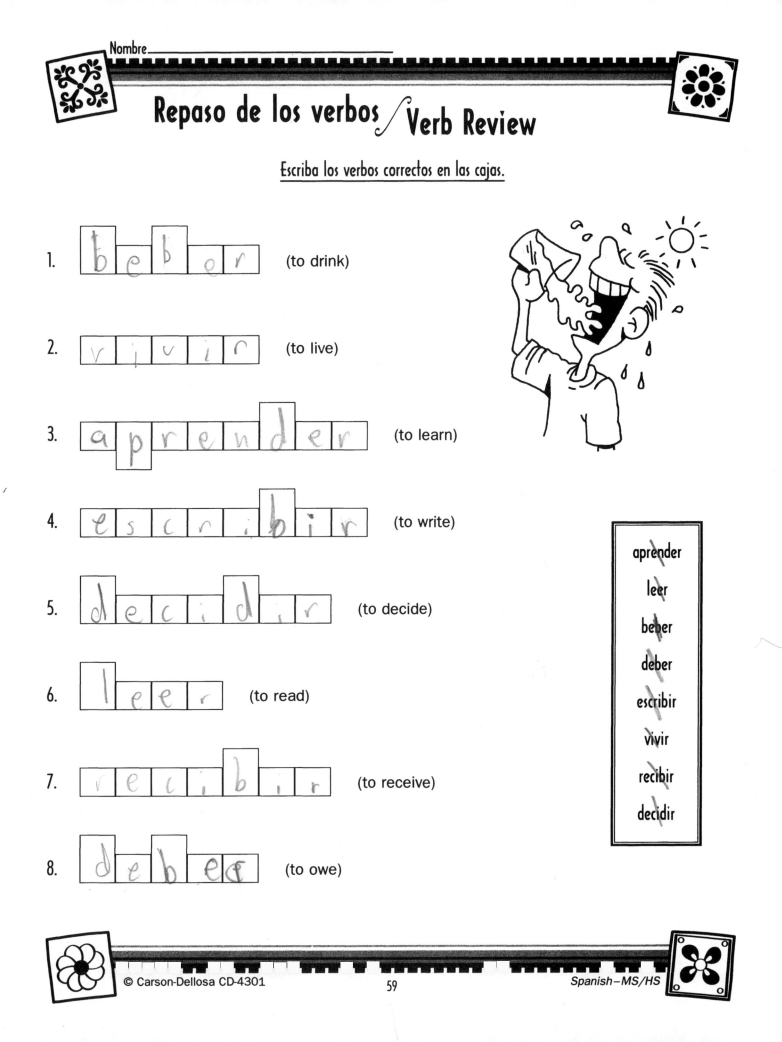

1. b e b e r (to drink)

2. v i v i r (to live)

3. a p r e n d e r (to learn)

4. e s c r i b i r (to write)

5. d e c i d i r (to decide)

6. l e e r (to read)

7. r e c i b i r (to receive)

8. d e b e r (to owe)

aprender
leer
beber
deber
escribir
vivir
recibir
decidir

Usando los verbos / Using Verbs

Escriba las formas correctas de los verbos en las líneas.
Write the correct forms of the verbs on the lines.

1. Mi familia _____viaja_____ a California cada invierno.
   My family travels to California every winter.

2. _____Visitamos_____ a la tía Ana y al tío Marco.
   We visit Aunt Ana and Uncle Marco.

3. _____Viven_____ en Santa Barbara.
   They live in Santa Barbara.

4. Mi hermano _____nada_____ todos los días.
   My brother swims every day.

5. _____Escribe_____ muchas cartas a mis amigas.
   I write lots of letters to my friends.

6. __Me ponge__ el traje de baño y _____camine_____ por la playa.
   I put on a swimsuit and walk along the beach.

7. _____Eschuche_____ las olas.
   I listen to the waves.

8. _____Como_____ mucho pescado y _____bebo_____ mucha agua.
   We eat lots of fish and drink lots of water.

9. Mi madre _____juega_____ al golf mientras mi padre _____lee_____ un libro.
   My mother plays golf while my father reads a book.

10. _____Compre_____ unos recuerdos para mis amigas.
    I buy some souvenirs for my friends.

leer	jugar	comprar	beber	ponerse	nadar	caminar
vivir	escribir	viajar		visitar	comer	escuchar

La negación / Negation

To negate a simple statement, put the word no in front of the verb.

Example: Él está listo.
Ella no está lista.

To answer a question in the negative, begin the sentence with No, and then repeat the no before the verb.

Example: ¿Estás listo?
No, no estoy listo.

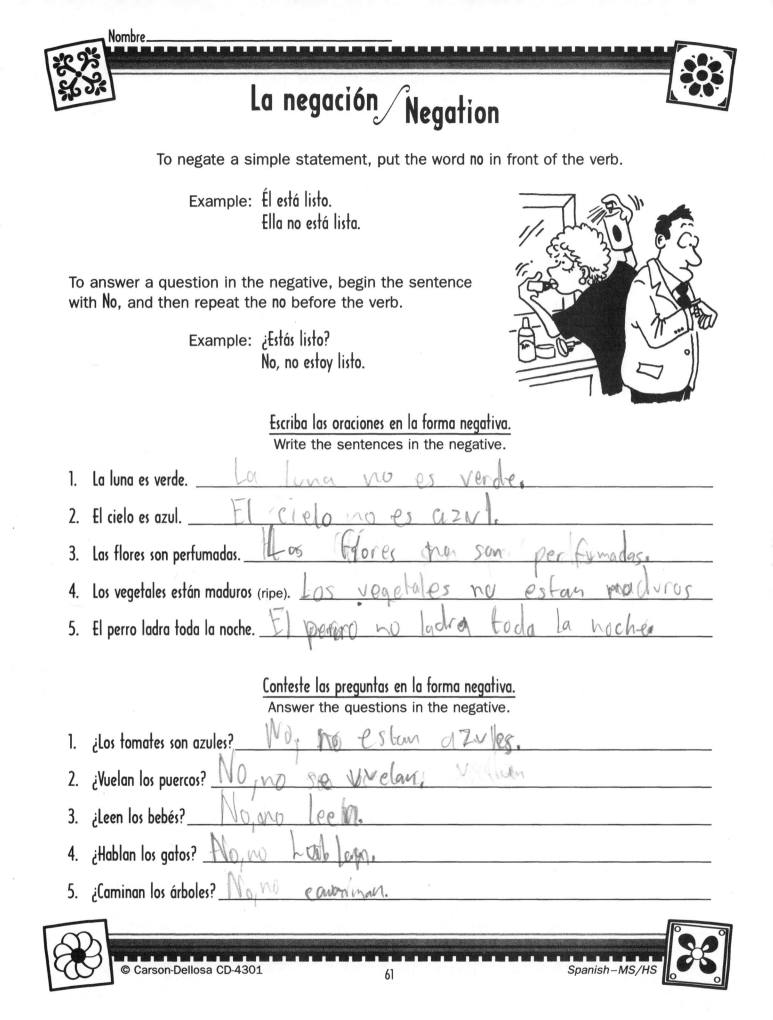

Escriba las oraciones en la forma negativa.
Write the sentences in the negative.

1. La luna es verde. _La luna no es verde._
2. El cielo es azul. _El cielo no es azul._
3. Las flores son perfumadas. _Las flores no son perfumadas._
4. Los vegetales están maduros (ripe). _Los vegetales no están maduros_
5. El perro ladra toda la noche. _El perro no ladra toda la noche_

Conteste las preguntas en la forma negativa.
Answer the questions in the negative.

1. ¿Los tomates son azules? _No, no están azules._
2. ¿Vuelan los puercos? _No, no se vuelan, vuelan_
3. ¿Leen los bebés? _No, no leen._
4. ¿Hablan los gatos? _No, no hablan._
5. ¿Caminan los árboles? _No, no caminan._

Tener / "To Have"

The verb tener is irregular. It does not follow the rules of conjugation.

Example: Ella tiene pelo largo. ....She has long hair.

This chart shows how to conjugate tener.

tener (to have)

yo	tengo	nosotros/-as	tenemos
tú	tienes	vosotros/-as	tenéis
él/ella/Ud.	tiene	ellos/ellas/Uds.	tienen

Conteste con "sí" o "no" en oraciones completas.
Answer with "yes" or "no" in complete sentences.

1. ¿Un hombre tiene cinco piernas? _No._____

2. ¿Una niña tiene dos brazos? _Sí._____

3. ¿Un niño tiene tres ojos? _No._____

4. ¿Tenemos veinte dedos de las manos? _No._____

5. ¿Tienes manos en la cabeza? _No._____

6. ¿El gato tiene dos narices? _No._____

7. ¿Ud. tiene diez dedos de los pies? _Sí._____

8. ¿Los animales tienen dos orejas? _Sí._____

9. ¿Una persona tiene dos bocas? _No._____

10. ¿Las jirafas tienen cuellos largos? _Sí._____

la pierna = leg	el dedo de la mano = finger	la cabeza = head
el brazo = arm	el dedo del pie = toe	la oreja = ear
el ojo = eye	la nariz = nose	la boca = mouth
el cuello = neck	largo = long	el pelo = hair

Otros usos de "tener" / Other Uses of "Tener"

Many expressions in Spanish use the verb tener.
They are used to express things such as age and physical conditions or sensations.

▸ tener...años = to be...years old
    Tengo catorce años.................................I am fourteen years old.

▸ tener hambre/sed = to be hungry/thirsty
    Cuando tiene hambre, necesita comida. ....When you're hungry, you need food.
    Cuando tiene sed, necesita agua.................When you're thirsty, you need water.

▸ tener sueño = to be tired
    Tengo sueño a la una de la madrugada. ....I am tired at 1:00 in the morning.

▸ tener calor/frío = to be hot/cold *
    En el verano, tengo calor. ....In the summer, I am hot.
    En el invierno, tengo frío........................In the winter, I am cold.

    (*Hacer calor/frío is used with weather. Estar caliente/frío is used with objects.)

▸ tener dolor de [body part] = to have an ache or to be sore
    Jaime tiene dolor de cabeza......................Jaime has a headache.

Escriba las oraciones en español.

1. We are not hungry.   Nosotros no tenemos hambre.

2. I am sixteen years old.   Tengo dieciséis

3. She is cold.   Ella tiene frío.

4. You (sing.) have a headache. Tu tienes un dolor de cabeza

5. The girls are tired.   Las niñas tienen suena

6. Are you (pl.) thirsty?   ¿Tu tienes sed?

Otros usos de "tener" / Other Uses of "Tener"

Here are some other expressions that include tener.

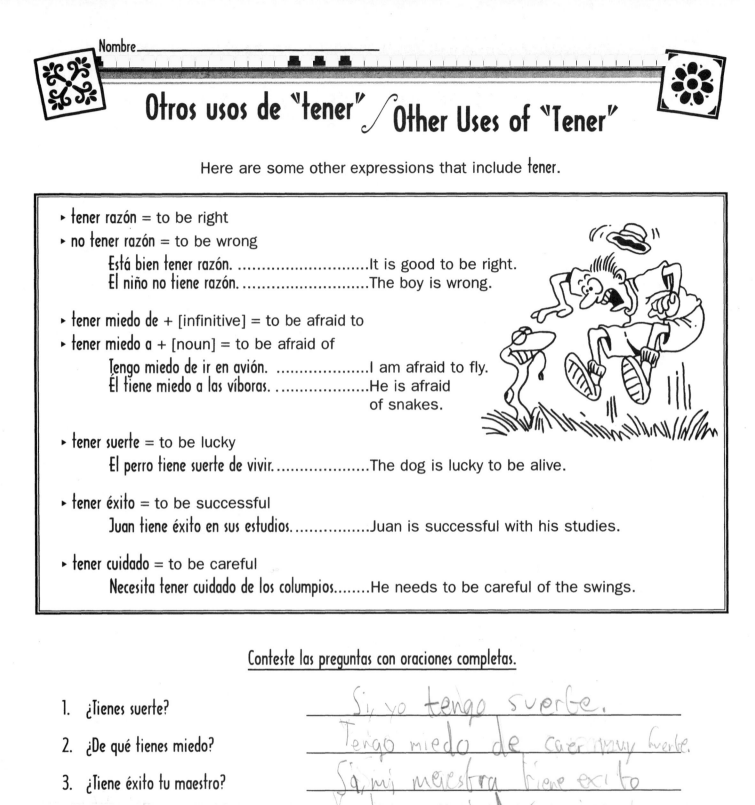

▸ tener razón = to be right

▸ no tener razón = to be wrong

  Está bien tener razón. ....It is good to be right.
  El niño no tiene razón. ....The boy is wrong.

▸ tener miedo de + [infinitive] = to be afraid to

▸ tener miedo a + [noun] = to be afraid of

  Tengo miedo de ir en avión. ....I am afraid to fly.
  Él tiene miedo a las víboras. ....He is afraid
               of snakes.

▸ tener suerte = to be lucky

  El perro tiene suerte de vivir....................The dog is lucky to be alive.

▸ tener éxito = to be successful

  Juan tiene éxito en sus estudios.................Juan is successful with his studies.

▸ tener cuidado = to be careful

  Necesita tener cuidado de los columpios........He needs to be careful of the swings.

Conteste las preguntas con oraciones completas.

1. ¿Tienes suerte?

  Si, yo tengo suerte.

2. ¿De qué tienes miedo?

  Tengo miedo de caer muy fuerte.

3. ¿Tiene éxito tu maestro?

  Si, mi maestra tiene exito

4. ¿A qué tienes miedo?

  Yo tengo miedo a injecsiones.

5. ¿Tienes siempre razón?

  Yo no siempre tengo razon

6. ¿Tienes cuidado con los bebés?

  Si, yo tengo cuidado con los bebes.

Tener que / "To Have To"

The phrase **tener que** + [infinitive] expresses a need or obligation to do something.

Examples: Ellos tienen que hacer su tarea. ....They have to do their homework.
Tengo que escribir una reseña sobre un libro......I have to write a book report.

Hay que + [infinitive] expresses a general necessity. There is no true subject.

Examples: Hay que estudiar cada día. ....It is necessary to study each day.
No hay que fumar en el restaurante. ....One shouldn't smoke in the restaurant.

Escriba las oraciones usando "tener que".

1. Paseo el perro.   (pasear = to walk)

   Tengo que pasear el perro.

2. Limpias la recámara.   (limpiar = to clean)

   Tengo que limpiar la recámara

3. Ustedes sacan la basura.   (sacar la basura = to take out the trash)

   Hay que sacar la basura

4. Ella corta el césped.   (cortar el césped = to mow the lawn)

   _____

5. Rastrillamos las hojas.   (rastrillar = to rake)

   Hay que rastrillamos las hojas

6. Él lava los platos.   (lavar = to wash)

   _____

Escriba la oración en español.

One must sweep the floor.   _Alguien necesita a barrer el piso._
(barrer el piso)

Repaso con "tener" / Review with "Tener"

Trace una línea entre la frase en español y la frase en inglés.

¿Cuántos años tienes?	I have cold hands.
Tenemos razón.	I am afraid to sing.
Ud. tiene cuidado con la bicicleta.	We are not hungry.
Tengo las manos frías.	I am hot.
¿Tienes miedo a los perros?	You are wrong.
Tengo mucho sueño.	How old are you?
No tienes razón.	Are you afraid of dogs?
Tengo calor.	I am very tired.
Tengo miedo de cantar.	You are careful with the bicycle.
No tenemos hambre.	We are right.

Escriba los nombres apropiados para completar las oraciones.

1. Hoy es mi cumpleaños. Tengo dieciséis _____.

   Today is my birthday. I am sixteen years old.

2. Es invierno y está nevando. Tengo _____.

   It is winter and it is snowing. I am cold.

3. Te ganaste la lotería. Tienes _____.

   You won the lottery. You are lucky.

4. Ella comió un desayuno grande. Ella no tiene _____.

   She ate a big breakfast. She is not hungry.

5. Nunca voy al cine. Tengo _____ a la oscuridad.

   I never go to the movies. I am afraid of the dark.

Más…que / More…Than

To compare two or more things in Spanish, use the phrase **más…que**.
The word **más** means "more." It can be used with adjectives, adverbs, or nouns.
Remember that adjectives must agree in gender and number with the nouns they modify.

Examples: **El elefante es más grande que el ratón.**
The elephant is bigger ("more big") than the mouse.

La niña corre más rápido que el niño.
The girl runs faster ("more fast") than the boy.

Tengo más hermanas que hermanos.
I have more sisters than brothers.

Escriba las oraciones en español.

1. _____
   Veronica is prettier than Lupe.

2. _____
   The sweater is uglier than the pants.

3. _____
   The cookies are sweeter than the cake.

4. _____
   My house is bigger than Gloria's house.

5. _____
   Vicente eats faster than Pedro.

bonito = pretty	la galleta = cookie	el pastel = cake	rápido = fast
feo = ugly	dulce = sweet	la casa = house	grande = big

Menos...que / Less...Than

To make a negative comparison, use the phrase **menos...que**.
The word **menos** means "less." This can be used with adjectives, adverbs, or nouns.
Remember that adjectives must agree in gender and number with the nouns they modify.

Examples: El pelo de Sandee es menos rizado que el pelo de Lisa.
   Sandee's hair is less curly than Lisa's hair.

   Tomás tiene menos dinero que su hermano.
   Tomás has less money than his brother.

Escriba las oraciones en español.

1. _____
   Maria is less tall than her sister.

2. _____
   Math is less interesting than science.

3. _____
   I have fewer brothers than sisters.

4. _____
   My sister is less hungry than my cousin.

las matemáticas = math	la ciencia = science	el hermano/la hermana = brother/sister
interesante = interesting	alto = tall	el primo/la prima = cousin

Escriba dos comparaciones con "menos...que".

1. _____

2. _____

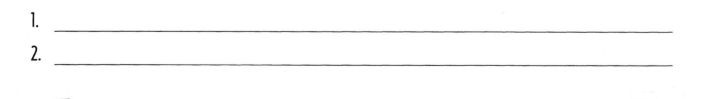

Tan...como / As...As

To make an equal comparison, use the phrase tan...como.

Examples: **Soy tan alto como mi amiga.**
I am as tall as my friend.

Marco corre tan rápido como Luisa.
Marco runs as fast as Luisa.

Tan remains unchanged before an adjective or adverb.
However, in front of a noun, it takes an ending to match
the noun in gender and number.

Examples: **Gasto tanto dinero como Isabel.**.....................I spend as much money as Isabel.
Tengo tantos libros como Anita.....................I have as many books as Anita.
Bebo tanta leche como Diego........................I drink as much milk as Diego.
Como tantas galletas como Ramón.................I eat as many cookies as Ramón.

Escriba las oraciones en español.

1. _____

Laura is as old as Benito.

2. _____

Mia is as pretty as Juana.

3. _____

I have as many dogs as Carmen.

4. _____

Roberto watches as much TV as Jorge.   (mirar la televisión = to watch TV)

5. _____

Girls run as fast as boys.

Las comparaciones / Comparisons

Some comparative adjectives and adverbs have their own unique forms.
These words are not combined with **más** or **menos** to form comparative statements.

Adjectives

mucho – más	much – more
poco – menos	little – less
bueno – mejor	good – better
malo – peor	bad – worse
grande – mayor	old (big) – older
pequeño – menor	young (small) – younger

Adverbs

mucho – más	much – more
poco – menos	little – less
bien – mejor	well – better
mal – peor	badly – worse

but...

grande – más grande	big (size) – bigger
pequeño – más pequeño	small (size) – smaller

Examples: **Martina es menor que su hermana.**
Martina is younger than her sister.

Juego al golf peor que juego al fútbol.
I play golf worse than I play soccer.

Carl es un mejor escalador que yo.
Carl is a better climber than I am.

<u>Escriba las oraciones en español.</u>

1. _____

   You have more money than I do.

2. _____

   I am older than my sister.

3. _____

   Cecilia is a better student than Kim.

4. _____

   Martin's grades are worse than Kevin's grades.   (las notas = grades)

Las comparaciones / Comparisons

Escriba las oraciones en español usando el vocabulario.

1. The owl is larger than the mouse.   el búho / grande / el ratón

   _____

2. She is as pretty as a flower.   ella / bonito / la flor

   _____

3. He is taller than the teacher.   él / alto / el maestro

   _____

4. The book is heavier than the rock.   el libro / pesado / la roca

   _____

5. I am less hungry than you are.   yo / tener hambre / tú

   _____

6. I have as many books as Sita does.   yo / los libros / Sita

   _____

7. Dogs are louder than rabbits.
   los perros / ruidoso / los conejos

   _____

   _____

8. The ant is smaller than the beetle.
   la hormiga / pequeño / el escarabajo

   _____

   _____

Querer / "To Want"

Querer is an irregular verb that means "to want." Look at the chart to see how it is conjugated.

querer (to want)

yo	quiero	nosotros/-as	queremos
tú	quieres	vosotros/-as	queréis
él/ella/Ud.	quiere	ellos/ellas/Uds.	quieren

Escriba las frases en español.

I want _____

she wants _____

you (pl.) want _____

we want _____

they want _____

you (sing.) want _____

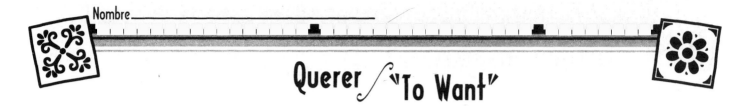

¿Qué quieres para tu cumpleaños? Escriba las oraciones completas.
What do you want for your birthday? Write complete sentences.

1. yo / una computadora nueva _____

2. tú / un estéreo _____

3. nosotros / mucho dinero _____

4. usted / una bicicleta _____

5. ellos / un perro _____

6. ella / un collar de oro _____

¿Que quieres hacer? / What Do You Want to Do?

The verb **querer** can be used with another verb to convey the desire to do something.
The verb that follows is always in the infinitive.

Example: Él quiere ir a la playa...........He wants to go to the beach.

Escriba las oraciones en inglés.

Queremos dormir. _____

Ellos quieren cantar. _____

Ella quiere nadar. _____

Él quiere bailar. _____

No quiero hacer la tarea. _____

Quieres comer. _____

Escriba las oraciones en español.

1. I want to read a book.

   _____

2. He wants to speak Spanish.

   _____

3. We want to play tennis.

   _____

4. She wants to play the guitar.

   _____

5. You (pl.) want to buy a new car.

   _____

6. They want to listen to the radio.

   _____

Ir / "To Go"

Learn how to conjugate the verb ir.

ir (to go)

yo	voy	nosotros/-as	vamos
tú	vas	vosotros/-as	vais
él/ella/Ud.	va	ellos/ellas/Uds.	van

Escriba las frases en español.

I go _____ you (pl.) go _____

the boys go _____ we go _____

you (sing.) go _____ she goes _____

¿A dónde van las personas? Escriba las oraciones en español.

Example: Quiero comprar unas frutas.   *Voy al supermercado.*

1. Ella quiere ver los árboles.

   _____

2. Queremos dinero.

   _____

3. Quieres enviar una carta.

   _____

4. Quiero comprar una chaqueta.

   _____

5. Ustedes quieren viajar a Australia.

   _____

6. Usted quiere ver una película (a film).

   _____

> ► ir al aeropuerto
> to go to the airport
>
> ► ir al banco
> to go to the bank
>
> ► ir al cine
> to go to the movies
>
> ► ir de compras
> to go shopping
>
> ► ir al correo
> to go to the post office
>
> ► ir al parque
> to go to the park

Voy a . . . / I am going to (+ verb) . . .

The verb ir can be used with an infinitive to describe an action that is planned for the future. Always use the preposition a between the two verbs: ir (conjugated) + a + [infinitive]. It is similar to the "I am going to (+ verb) . . ." structure in English.

Examples: Voy a decidir. ....I am going to decide.
Vamos a hacer la tarea. .....We are going to do the homework.
Van a bailar. ....They are going to dance.

Complete las oraciones. Escriba las frases en español.

1. _____ mi libro.
   I am going to read

2. _____ con tu amiga.
   You are going to talk

3. _____ en el parque mañana.
   We are going to play

4. _____ mi chaqueta en el frío.
   I am going to wear

Escriba cada oración usando el verbo ir y el infinitivo.

1. Leo un libro.
   _____

2. Ella llama a su amiga.
   _____

3. Jugamos en el parque.
   _____

4. Miras la televisión.
   _____

5. Ustedes visitan a sus abuelos.
   _____

6. Ellos manejan a Chicago.
   _____

¿Sí o no? / Yes or No?

As you already know, questions in Spanish are surrounded by question marks. The order of the words in a question may vary without changing the meaning.

Example: ¿Carmina tiene muchos animales?
¿Tiene Carmina muchos animales?
Does Carmina have lots of animals?

Escriba cada oración como una pregunta.

1. Los perros ladran mucho.   _____

2. El gato es simpático.   _____

3. Las vacas comen todo el día.   _____

Conteste las preguntas.

1. ¿La vaca come pasto (grass)?   _____

2. ¿Puede el puerco volar?   _____

Escriba una pregunta para cada respuesta.

1. _____

Sí, tengo cinco perros.

2. _____

No, no tengo borregos.

3. _____

Sí, sé andar a caballo.

4. _____

Sí, vivo en la granja.

¿Qué? / What?

The word **qué** means "what" in English. The question form always has an accent.
In a question, the word **qué** is followed by the verb.
The question **qué** is always answered with an object or an activity—never a person.

Examples: ¿Qué haces? ....What are you doing?
              ¿Qué tiene Ud.? ....What do you have?
              ¿Qué dice Ramón? ....What does Ramón say?

Escriba las preguntas en inglés.

1. _____

  ¿Qué escribes?

2. _____

  ¿Qué tienes que hacer?

3. _____

  ¿Qué comes?

4. _____

  ¿Qué dice la niña?

5. _____

  ¿Qué quieres hacer?

6. _____

  ¿Qué lees?

7. _____

  ¿Qué practican ustedes? (practice)

8. _____

  ¿Qué escuchan los niños?

¿Qué? / What?

Escriba la pregunta apropiada usando "qué".

1. Tengo un vestido nuevo. ¿Qué tienes?

2. Escuchamos la música de Brasil. _____

3. Juegan con sus amigos esta tarde. _____

4. La lección es la de la página dos. _____

5. Son mis libros. _____

6. Como una hamburguesa. _____

7. Él lee una revista. _____

8. Miramos los dibujos animados (cartoons). _____

9. La niña pinta un dibujo de los árboles. _____

10. Ella hace galletas. _____

Trace una línea entre la pregunta y la respuesta apropiada.

¿Qué comen los niños?   Yo leo un libro.

¿Qué llevas?   Nosotros escribimos una carta.

¿Qué lees?   Está nevando.

¿Qué escriben?   Ellos comen unas fresas.

¿Qué tiempo hace?   Llevo un suéter nuevo.

¿Qué hora es? / What Time Is It?

To ask what time it is in Spanish, say ¿Qué hora es?
To answer, say Son las and the number of the hour.
One o'clock is expressed: Es la una.

Examples: ¿Qué hora es? ....What time is it?
Es la una. ....It is one o'clock.
Son las dos. ....It is two o'clock.

Add minutes to the current hour up to 30 minutes. Use the word y.
After 30, subtract the minutes from the next hour. Use the word menos.

Examples: Son las seis y diez. ....It is 6:10.
Son las tres menos diez. ......It is 2:50. (three minus ten)

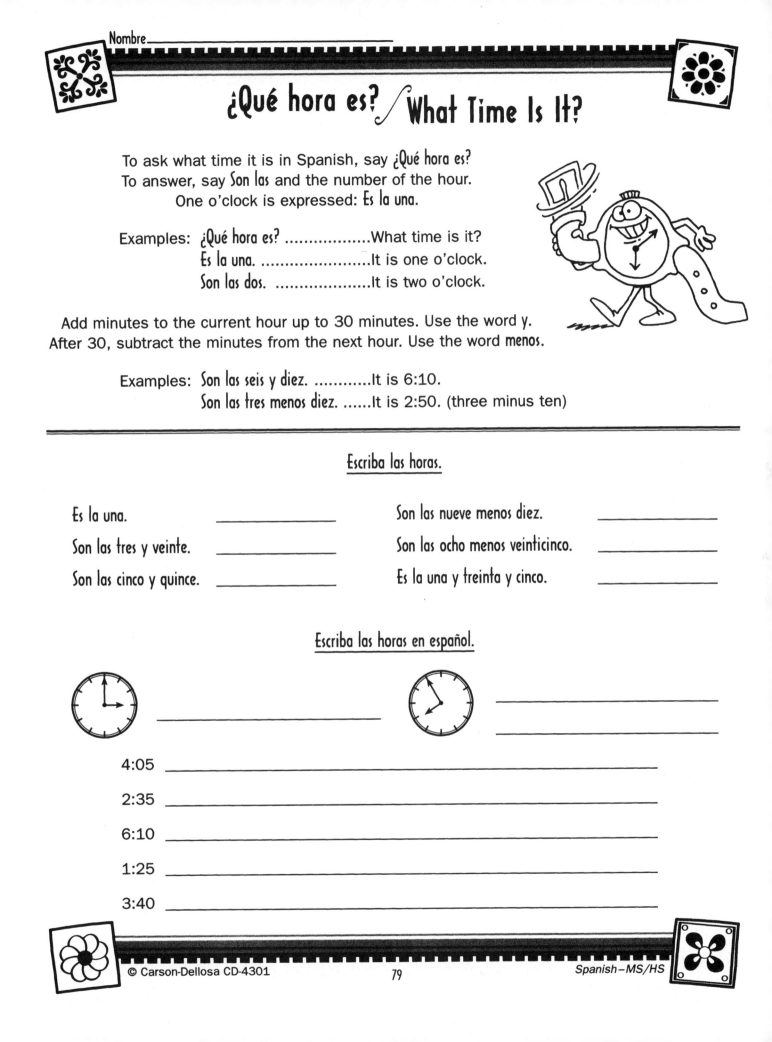

Escriba las horas.

Es la una.   _____

Son las tres y veinte.   _____

Son las cinco y quince.   _____

Son las nueve menos diez.   _____

Son las ocho menos veinticinco. _____

Es la una y treinta y cinco. _____

Escriba las horas en español.

_____

_____

4:05 _____

2:35 _____

6:10 _____

1:25 _____

3:40 _____

¿Qué hora es? / What Time Is It?

Here are some other common time expressions.

10:00 ....Son las diez <u>en punto</u> (on the dot).
12:15 ....Son las doce <u>y cuarto</u> (quarter).
7:30 ....Son las siete <u>y media</u> (half).
5:45 ....Son las seis <u>menos cuarto</u>.

<u>Escriba las horas.</u>

Es la una y media. _____   Son las nueve menos cuarto. _____

Son las once y cuarto. _____   Son las cuatro en punto. _____

de la madrugada = in the morning (very early)	de la tarde = in the afternoon
de la mañana = in the morning	de la noche = in the evening / at night

<u>Escriba las horas en español.</u>

4:15 _____

2:30 _____

6:08 _____

1:23 A.M. _____

4:45 P.M. _____

<u>Trace una línea entre la hora y la frase correcta en español.</u>

3:00	Es la una menos cuarto.
1:15	Son las tres y media.
12:45	Son las doce y cuarto.
3:30	Son las tres en punto.
12:15	Es la una y cuarto.

¿A qué hora? / At What Time?

To ask when or at what time, say ¿A qué hora?
To reply, say A and then the time.

Example: ¿A qué hora vamos al cine? ....When (at what time) are we going to the movie?
Vamos a las siete.....................We are going at seven o'clock.

Conteste las preguntas en español.

1. ¿A qué hora comes el desayuno? (breakfast)

_____

2. ¿A qué hora comes el almuerzo? (lunch)

_____

3. ¿A qué hora comes la cena? (dinner)

_____

4. ¿A qué hora sales para la escuela?

_____

Dibuje las manos en los relojes.
Draw the hands on the clocks.

Es la una y cinco.   Son las ocho y cincuenta.   Son las tres menos cuarto.   Son las doce y veinte.

Son las siete y diez.   Son las cinco y media.   Son las cuatro menos diez.   Es la una en punto.

¿Quién? / Who?

Quién means "who."

Example: ¿Quién fue el decimosexto presidente de los Estados Unidos?
Who was the sixteenth president of the United States?

Escriba las preguntas con "quién" usando las frases.

1. pintar los dibujos
   (to paint pictures)
   ¿Quién pinta los dibujos? _____

2. manejar los carros
   (to drive cars)
   _____

3. trabajar con los dientes
   (to work with teeth)
   _____

4. cuidar de tu salud
   (to take care of your health)
   _____

5. arreglar los carros
   (to fix cars)
   _____

6. cocinar la comida
   (to cook food)
   _____

7. repartir el correo
   (to deliver the mail)
   _____

8. cultivar los alimentos
   (to grow food)
   _____

9. escribir libros
   (to write books)
   _____

Escriba el número de la pregunta al lado de la mejor respuesta.

el mecánico _____   el cocinero _____   el cartero _____   el granjero _____   la autora _____

la artista _____   el chofer _____   la dentista _____   el doctor _____

¿Dónde? / Where?

Dónde means "where." The answer is always a location.

Example: ¿Dónde está la pelota? ....Where is the ball?
Está abajo de la mesa..............It is under the table.

Conteste las preguntas en oraciones completas.

1. ¿Dónde está tu sombrero?
   _____
   on my head

2. ¿Dónde está la cafetería?
   _____
   behind the gym   (el gimnasio)

3. ¿Dónde está el gato?
   _____
   in front of the school

4. ¿Dónde está la pelota?
   _____
   inside the closet   (el ropero)

5. ¿Dónde está su abuela?
   _____
   outside in the garden   (el jardín)

6. ¿Dónde está el libro?
   _____
   next to the pencil

7. ¿Dónde está el avión?
   _____
   above the trees

---

sobre = on	atrás de = behind
en = in	afuera = outside
dentro de = inside of	encima de = over/above
al lado de = next to	enfrente de = in front of

¿Cuándo? / When?

Both cuándo and a qué hora are used to ask "when?"
Cuándo can be used to ask a specific or a more general time.
A qué hora is used only to ask a specific time of day.

Examples: ¿Cuándo comes el desayuno?   Como el desayuno en la mañana.
          ¿A qué hora comes el desayuno?   Como el desayuno a las ocho.

Escriba las oraciones en español o en inglés.

1. ¿Cuándo va él a México?   _____

2. ¿A qué hora partimos?   _____

3. _____   What time is dinner?

4. _____   When can we visit Marta?

5. ¿Cuándo vas al banco?   _____

6. _____   When is your birthday?

Escriba "cuándo" o "a qué hora" para completar las oraciones.

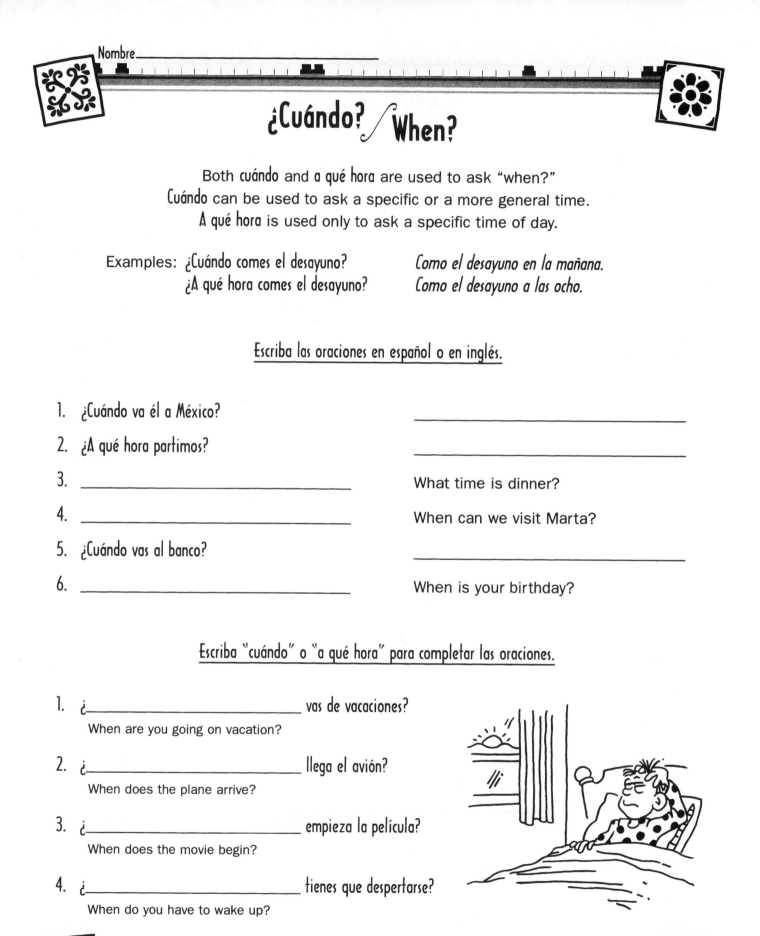

1. ¿_____ vas de vacaciones?
   When are you going on vacation?

2. ¿_____ llega el avión?
   When does the plane arrive?

3. ¿_____ empieza la película?
   When does the movie begin?

4. ¿_____ tienes que despertarse?
   When do you have to wake up?

¿Dónde? / Where?

Dónde means "where." The answer is always a location.

Example: ¿Dónde está la pelota? ....Where is the ball?
Está abajo de la mesa.............It is under the table.

Conteste las preguntas en oraciones completas.

1. ¿Dónde está tu sombrero?

   _____
   on my head

2. ¿Dónde está la cafetería?

   _____
   behind the gym   (el gimnasio)

3. ¿Dónde está el gato?

   _____
   in front of the school

4. ¿Dónde está la pelota?

   _____
   inside the closet   (el ropero)

5. ¿Dónde está su abuela?

   _____
   outside in the garden   (el jardín)

6. ¿Dónde está el libro?

   _____
   next to the pencil

7. ¿Dónde está el avión?

   _____
   above the trees

---

sobre = on	atrás de = behind
en = in	afuera = outside
dentro de = inside of	encima de = over/above
al lado de = next to	enfrente de = in front of

¿Cuándo? / When?

Both cuándo and a qué hora are used to ask "when?"
Cuándo can be used to ask a specific or a more general time.
A qué hora is used only to ask a specific time of day.

Examples: ¿Cuándo comes el desayuno?   Como el desayuno en la mañana.
                   ¿A qué hora comes el desayuno?   Como el desayuno a las ocho.

Escriba las oraciones en español o en inglés.

1. ¿Cuándo va él a México?   _____

2. ¿A qué hora partimos?   _____

3. _____   What time is dinner?

4. _____   When can we visit Marta?

5. ¿Cuándo vas al banco?   _____

6. _____   When is your birthday?

Escriba "cuándo" o "a qué hora" para completar las oraciones.

1. ¿_____ vas de vacaciones?
    When are you going on vacation?

2. ¿_____ llega el avión?
    When does the plane arrive?

3. ¿_____ empieza la película?
    When does the movie begin?

4. ¿_____ tienes que despertarse?
    When do you have to wake up?

¿Cuál? / Which?

The word cuál means "which."
Use cuál to ask about a singular noun and cuáles to ask about a plural noun.

Examples: ¿Cuál es tu camisa favorita? ....Which is your favorite shirt?
¿Cuáles son tus pantalones nuevos? ....Which are your new pants?

<u>Escriba "cuál" o "cuáles" en cada pregunta.</u>

1. ¿_____ es tu restaurante favorito?

2. ¿_____ de los hermanos es el mayor?

3. ¿_____ son los libros de Mónica?

4. ¿_____ es la mejor manzana?

<u>Conteste las preguntas usando "este/esta" (this) o "estos/estas" (those).</u>

1. ¿Cuál es mi vaso?

_____

2. ¿Cuáles son tus zapatos?

_____

3. ¿Cuál es su casa?

_____

4. ¿Cuál de los gatos se llama Max?

_____

5. ¿Cuáles son las llaves del carro?   (la llave = key)

_____

6. ¿Cuál de los discos compactos quieres escuchar?

_____

¿Cuánto? / How Much?

Cuánto/a is used to ask "how much?" Cuántos/as is used to ask "how many?"
It must agree in gender and number with the noun it modifies.

Examples: ¿Cuánto café quieres?......................How much coffee would you like?
¿Cuántas galletas puedes comer?.........How many cookies can you eat?

The question ¿Cuánto cuesta? means "How much does it cost?"

Escriba la forma correcta de "cuánto" en cada pregunta.

1. ¿_____ leche bebes?

2. ¿_____ queso puede él comer?

3. ¿_____ cuesta la comida?

4. ¿_____ manzanas hay?

5. ¿_____ cuestan las papas fritas?

Escriba una pregunta para cada respuesta.

1. Él tiene diecisiete años.

_____

2. Hay veinte delfines al lado del barco.

_____

3. Cuesta doscientos dólares.

_____

4. No tengo ni hermanos ni hermanas.

_____

5. Podemos comprar dos videos.

_____

Nombre_____

¿Cuál? / Which?

The word cuál means "which."
Use cuál to ask about a singular noun and cuáles to ask about a plural noun.

Examples: ¿Cuál es tu camisa favorita? ....Which is your favorite shirt?
¿Cuáles son tus pantalones nuevos? ....Which are your new pants?

<u>Escriba "cuál" o "cuáles" en cada pregunta.</u>

1. ¿_____ es tu restaurante favorito?
2. ¿_____ de los hermanos es el mayor?
3. ¿_____ son los libros de Mónica?
4. ¿_____ es la mejor manzana?

<u>Conteste las preguntas usando "este/esta"</u> (this) o "estos/estas" (those).

1. ¿Cuál es mi vaso?

_____

2. ¿Cuáles son tus zapatos?

_____

3. ¿Cuál es su casa?

_____

4. ¿Cuál de los gatos se llama Max?

_____

5. ¿Cuáles son las llaves del carro?   (la llave = key)

_____

6. ¿Cuál de los discos compactos quieres escuchar?

_____

¿Cuánto? / How Much?

Cuánto/a is used to ask "how much?" Cuántos/as is used to ask "how many?"
It must agree in gender and number with the noun it modifies.

Examples: ¿Cuánto café quieres?......................How much coffee would you like?
¿Cuántas galletas puedes comer?.........How many cookies can you eat?

The question ¿Cuánto cuesta? means "How much does it cost?"

Escriba la forma correcta de "cuánto" en cada pregunta.

1. ¿_____ leche bebes?

2. ¿_____ queso puede él comer?

3. ¿_____ cuesta la comida?

4. ¿_____ manzanas hay?

5. ¿_____ cuestan las papas fritas?

Escriba una pregunta para cada respuesta.

1. Él tiene diecisiete años.

_____

2. Hay veinte delfines al lado del barco.

_____

3. Cuesta doscientos dólares.

_____

4. No tengo ni hermanos ni hermanas.

_____

5. Podemos comprar dos videos.

_____

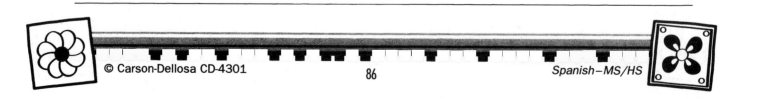

¿Cómo? y ¿por qué? / How? and Why?

Use the word **cómo** to ask "how?"

Examples: ¿Cómo trepas el árbol? ....How do you climb the tree?
¿Cómo se llama usted? ....What is your name?
(How do you call yourself?)

Trace una línea entre la pregunta en español y la pregunta en inglés.

¿Cómo se dice "hello" en español?   How are you doing?

¿Cómo te llamas?   How does he know the answer?

¿Cómo se juega al fútbol?   What is your name?

¿Cómo estás?   How do you spell your name?

¿Cómo sabe él la respuesta?   How do you play soccer?

¿Cómo se escribe tu nombre?   How do you say "hello" in Spanish?

Use the phrase **por qué** to ask "why?"

Examples: ¿Por qué está ella aquí? ....Why is she here?
¿Por qué estás triste?..............Why are you sad?

Escriba las preguntas en español.

1. Why is the sky blue?   _____

2. Why are you nervous?   _____

3. Why are they crying?   _____

4. Why is she leaving?   _____

5. Why are your hands green?   _____

6. Why aren't you eating?   _____

Repaso con preguntas / Review with Questions

Escriba las palabras correctas para completar las oraciones.

1. ¿_____ estás?

2. ¿_____ te llamas?

3. ¿_____ es el hombre al lado de Ana?

4. ¿_____ personas están en la fiesta?

5. ¿_____ años tiene Nico?

6. ¿_____ es tu cumpleaños?

7. ¿_____ está la comida? ¿En la cocina?

8. ¿_____ está nervioso Felipe?

9. ¿_____ vas a salir de la fiesta?

10. ¿_____ disco compacto está tocando?

11. Hay muchos regalos.

   ¿_____ está en la caja grande?

¡Feliz cumpleaños!

qué	cuál	por qué
quién	cuánto	a qué hora
dónde	cómo	cuándo

Escriba el número de la pregunta al lado de la mejor respuesta.

A. A las nueve y media. _____

B. Él se llama David. _____

C. Hay treinta personas. _____

D. Me llamo Paula. _____

E. Más o menos. ¿Y tú? _____

F. Tiene diecisiete años. _____

G. El trece de junio. _____

H. No, en el comedor. _____

I. Él no sabe bailar. _____

J. Es una bicicleta. _____

Una entrevista / An Interview

Conteste las preguntas.

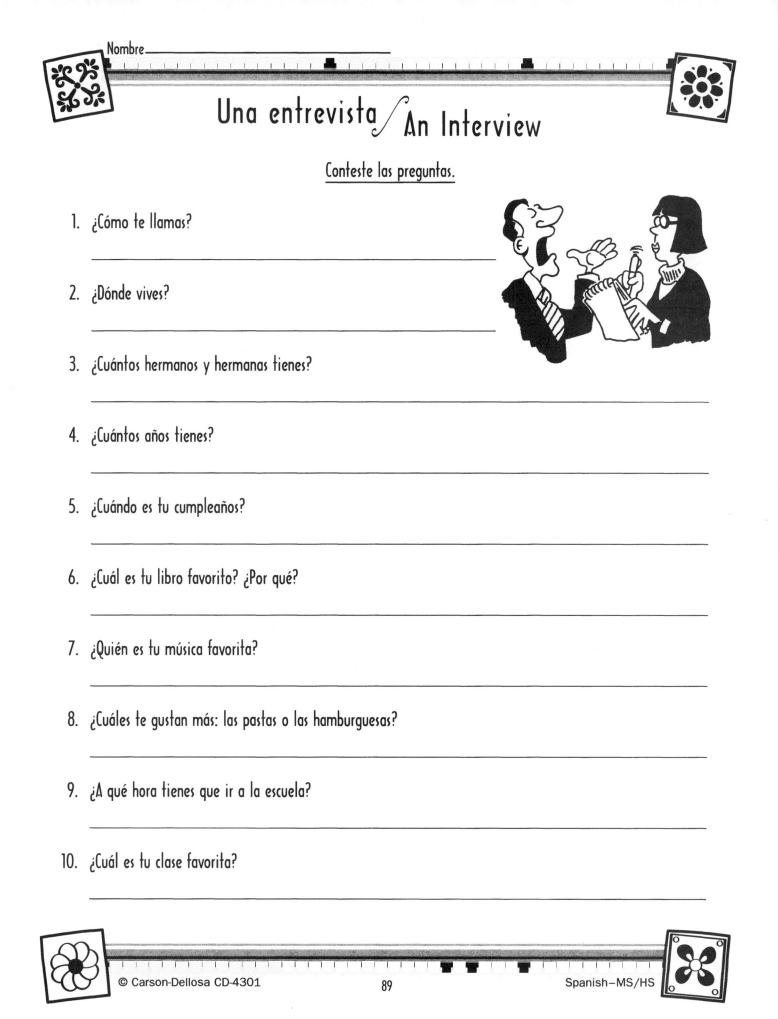

1. ¿Cómo te llamas?

   _____

2. ¿Dónde vives?

   _____

3. ¿Cuántos hermanos y hermanas tienes?

   _____

4. ¿Cuántos años tienes?

   _____

5. ¿Cuándo es tu cumpleaños?

   _____

6. ¿Cuál es tu libro favorito? ¿Por qué?

   _____

7. ¿Quién es tu música favorita?

   _____

8. ¿Cuáles te gustan más: las pastas o las hamburguesas?

   _____

9. ¿A qué hora tienes que ir a la escuela?

   _____

10. ¿Cuál es tu clase favorita?

    _____

Me gusta... / I Like...

Use the expression Me gusta followed by a noun to say that you like something in Spanish. Literally, it means, "It is pleasing to me [the noun]." Me gusta can also be used in front an infinitive verb to state "I like to [do something]."

Examples: Me gusta el dulce. ....I like candy.
Me gustan los perros...................I like dogs.
Me gusta viajar. ....I like to travel.

This chart shows the proper pronouns to use before gusta(n).
Use **gusta** with singular nouns and verbs and **gustan** for plural nouns.

me gusta(n)	I like	nos gusta(n)	we like
te gusta(n)	you (sing.) like	os gusta(n)	you (pl.) like
le gusta(n)	he/she likes, you (form.) like	les gusta(n)	they/you (pl.) like

Escriba las oraciones en español.

1. I like your watch. (el reloj)

   Me gusta el reloj.

2. We like coffee. (el café)

   Nos gustan el café.

3. He likes the shirt. (la camisa)

   Le gusta la camisa

4. He likes to dance. (bailar) _____

5. We like vacations. (las vacaciones) _____

6. She likes to listen to music. (la música) _____

7. You (sing.) like to read books. (los libros) _____

8. They like the cake. (el pastel) _____

(No) me gusta... / I (Don't) Like...

State whether you like or dislike the foods shown below.
Use Me gusta(n) or No me gusta(n).

Examples: Me gusta el helado.....................I like ice cream.
No me gustan las cebollas.............I don't like onions.

las frambuesas

las aceitunas

las manzanas

el pan

los guisantes

la sandía

1. _____.

2. _____.

3. _____.

4. _____.

5. _____.

6. _____.

7. _____.

8. _____.

9. _____.

10. _____.

11. _____.

12. _____.

los pepinos

las naranjas

los plátanos

el queso

los rábanos

el pescado

¿Qué les gusta más? / What Do They Prefer?

Escriba las respuestas en español.

Example: ¿Te gusta más el helado o el pastel?
Me gusta más el helado.

1. ¿Te gusta más una hamburguesa o un sándwich?

   _____

2. ¿A ustedes les gustan más las galletas o los vegetales?

   _____

3. ¿A ella le gustan más los pimientos o las cebollas?

   _____

4. ¿A usted le gusta más el café o la leche?

   _____

5. ¿Te gustan más las papas fritas o las papas al horno?

   _____

6. ¿A ustedes les gusta más la carne o el queso?

   _____

7. ¿A él le gusta más el pollo o el pescado?

   _____

Dar / "To Give"

The verb dar means "to give." It is an irregular verb. Learn its conjugation.

dar (to give)

yo	doy	nosotros/-as	damos
tú	das	vosotros/-as	dais
él/ella/Ud.	da	ellos/ellas/Uds.	dan

Escriba las frases en español.

I give	_____	she gives	_____
you (pl.) give	_____	we give	_____
they give	_____	you (sing.) give	_____

> To say that you give something to someone, use the phrase "dar a."

Examples: Él da las flores a su novia. ....He gives his girlfriend the flowers.
Damos el hueso al perro............We give the bone to the dog.

Escriba las oraciones en español.

1. I give the book to my brother.

   _____

2. You (sing.) give the teacher an apple.

   _____

3. We give the kids ice cream.

   _____

4. They give the keys to their mother.

   _____

> Use the contraction "al" in place of a + el.

Otros usos de "dar" / Other Uses of "Dar"

The verb dar is used in many expressions.
In these expressions, the verb takes on a different meaning.

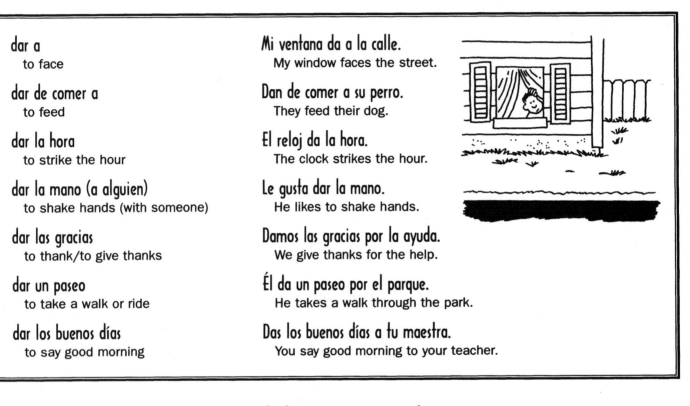

dar a
  to face

Mi ventana da a la calle.
  My window faces the street.

dar de comer a
  to feed

Dan de comer a su perro.
  They feed their dog.

dar la hora
  to strike the hour

El reloj da la hora.
  The clock strikes the hour.

dar la mano (a alguien)
  to shake hands (with someone)

Le gusta dar la mano.
  He likes to shake hands.

dar las gracias
  to thank/to give thanks

Damos las gracias por la ayuda.
  We give thanks for the help.

dar un paseo
  to take a walk or ride

Él da un paseo por el parque.
  He takes a walk through the park.

dar los buenos días
  to say good morning

Das los buenos días a tu maestra.
  You say good morning to your teacher.

Escriba las oraciones en español.

1. Our house faces the street.

_____

2. I shake hands with my neighbor.

(**el vecino** = neighbor)

_____

3. He says thanks for the cookies.

_____

4. We take a walk after dinner.

_____

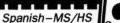

Practica con "dar" / Practice with "Dar"

Escriba la frase correcta para completar cada oración.

1. Cada día al mediodía, el reloj _____.
   Every day at noon, the clock strikes the hour.

2. Para el desayuno, mi mamá me _____ huevos.
   For breakfast, my mother feeds me eggs.

3. La maestra siempre _____ a la clase.
   The teacher always says good morning to the class.

4. El sofá en la sala _____ la puerta.
   The sofa in the living room faces the door.

5. El hombre _____ a la señorita.
   The man shakes the young woman's hand.

6. Es bueno _____ cuando se recibe un regalo.
   It is good to say thank you for a present.

7. Me gusta _____ por el parque.
   I like to walk through the park.

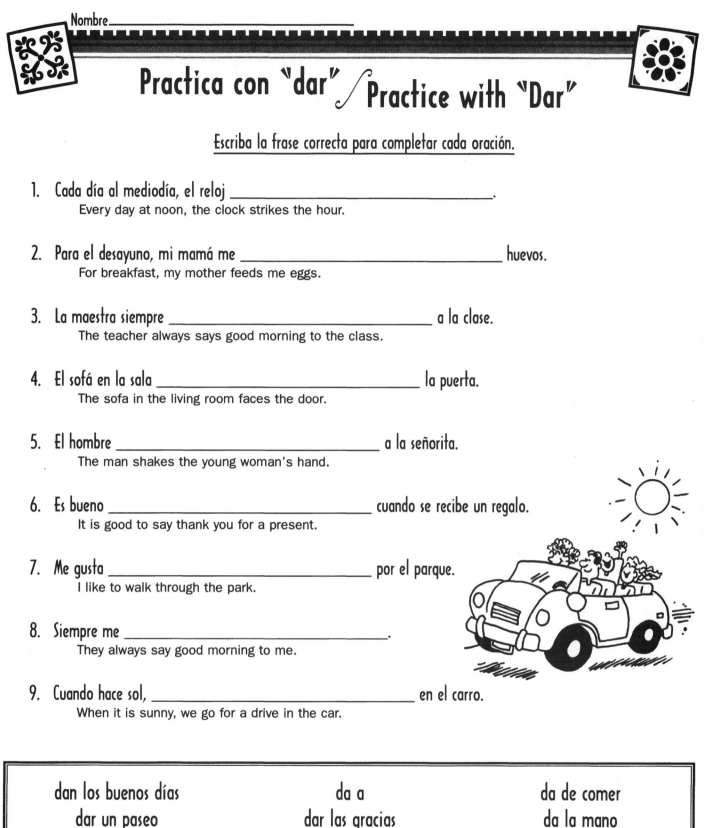

8. Siempre me _____.
   They always say good morning to me.

9. Cuando hace sol, _____ en el carro.
   When it is sunny, we go for a drive in the car.

dan los buenos días	da a	da de comer
dar un paseo	dar las gracias	da la mano
da la hora	da los buenos días	damos un paseo

Saber y conocer / "To Know"

The verbs **saber** and **conocer** both mean "to know," but they are used in different situations.
Saber is used to express knowledge of facts or specific information.
Conocer is used to express familiarity with a person, place, or concept.

Examples:
Yo sé la respuesta. ....I know the answer.
¿Sabes donde está? ....Do you know where it is?
Yo conozco al Sr. Rodríguez. ....I know Mr. Rodríguez.*
Conocemos bien la ciudad. ....We know the city well.

saber (to know as a fact)

yo	sé	nosotros/-as	sabemos
tú	sabes	vosotros/-as	sabéis
él/ella/Ud.	sabe	ellos/ellas/Uds.	saben

conocer (to know someone/to be familiar with)

yo	conozco	nosotros/-as	conocemos
tú	conoces	vosotros/-as	conocéis
él/ella/Ud.	conoce	ellos/ellas/Uds.	conocen

* Note: When using the verb **conocer** you must use the preposition **a** before a person.

Escriba las frases en español.

	saber	conocer
I know	_____	_____
you (pl.) know	_____	_____
he knows	_____	_____
we know	_____	_____
you (sing.) know	_____	_____

Saber y conocer / "To Know"

<u>¿Sabe usted la diferencia entre "saber" y "conocer"? Trace un círculo alrededor del verbo correcto.</u>

1. ¿Tú **sabes / conoces** la ciudad bien?

2. Yo **sé / conozco** su dirección.

3. **Sabemos / Conocemos** España.

4. Él **sabe / conoce** hablar español.

5. ¿ **Saben / Conocen** ustedes a mi amiga Penélope?

<u>Escriba la forma correcta del verbo "saber" o "conocer" para completar cada oración.</u>

1. ¿Tú _____ el restaurante?

2. Sí, pero yo no _____ dónde está.

3. Ellos _____ la ciudad mejor que nosotros.

4. ¿Tú _____ el número de teléfono?

5. ¿Tú _____ si la biblioteca está abierta hoy?

6. ¿Tú _____ cuándo viene el próximo autobús?

7. Yo no _____ si el restaurante está lejos del hotel.

8. ¿Tú _____ el nuevo museo de arte moderno?

la ciudad = city
el autobús = bus
el hotel = hotel
el museo = museum
la biblioteca = library
el restaurante = restaurant
lejos = far

Poder ✓ "To Be Able To"

The word **poder** means "can" or "to be able to" in English.
It is used in front of another verb.

poder (to be able to/can)

yo	puedo	nosotros/-as	podemos
tú	puedes	vosotros/-as	podéis
él/ella/Ud.	puede	ellos/ellas/Uds.	pueden

When **poder** is used with another verb, the verb that follows must be in the infinitive form.

Examples: ¿Puedes correr rápido?........................Can you run fast?
Sí, puedo correr rápido. ....Yes, I can run fast.
No, no puedo correr rápido. ....No, I can't run fast.

Escriba las formas correctas de "poder" en las líneas.

ellos _____   ella _____

yo _____   tú _____

ustedes _____   nosotros _____

Escriba las frases en español.

1. You can write. _____

2. They (fem.) can eat. _____

3. We can learn. _____

4. You (pl.) can sing. _____

5. He can run fast. _____

6. I can make bread. _____

Poder / "To Be Able To"

Conteste las preguntas en oraciones completas.

1. ¿Puedes manejar un carro? _____

2. ¿Puedes pintar una jirafa? _____

3. ¿Puedes cocinar el desayuno? _____

4. ¿Puedes correr en la calle (in the street)? _____

5. ¿Puedes mirar la televisión? _____

Escriba las preguntas apropiadas.

1. Sí, puedo hacer tacos. _____

2. No, ella no puede nadar bien. _____

3. No, ustedes no pueden montar un león. _____

4. Sí, él puede pintar un dibujo de la escuela. _____

5. No, no podemos ir al cine. _____

¿Puede completar las oraciones?

1. ¿Qué _____ esta tarde?
   can we do

2. ¿_____ al parque?
   can you go

3. Sí, pero _____ mi bicicleta.
   I can't find

4. ¡No hay problema! _____.
   I can drive

El infinitivo / The Infinitive

In English, the gerund (or "ing" form of the verb) is used after some prepositions.
In Spanish, the infinitive is used instead.

Examples: sin pensar ....without thinking
al escuchar ....upon hearing

| sin = without | al = upon | antes de = before | después de = after |

Escriba las frases en español.

without doing _____   before washing _____

upon seeing _____   without seeing _____

after eating _____   upon reading _____

Complete las oraciones en español.

Contestó _____.
He answered without thinking.

Se lavó las manos _____.
She washed her hands before eating.

Escriba las oraciones en español.

1. She screams upon seeing a rat.

_____   (gritar = to scream)

2. They eat without talking.

_____

3. I read a book before leaving.

_____

4. We wash the dishes after eating.

_____

El infinitivo / The Infinitive

You have learned several verbs and verb phrases that always take the infinitive.
These include: tener que, hay que, gustar, and ir a.

tener que	**Tengo que limpiar mi recámara.** I have to clean my bedroom.
hay que	**Hay que estudiar mucho en la escuela.** You have to study a lot in school.
saber	**Él no sabe jugar al golf.** He does not know how to play golf.
gustar	**Me gusta comer helado.** I like to eat ice cream.
ir a	**Vamos a jugar béisbol.** We're going to play baseball.

Complete las oraciones con las frases apropiadas.

1. Fui a la escuela _____.
   I went to school without eating.

2. _____ la música.
   We like to listen to the music.

3. _____ a mi casa en la nieve.
   I have to walk home in the snow.

4. Para la buena salud, _____ vegetales y frutas.
   For good health, one must eat vegetables and fruits.

5. _____ una bicicleta nueva.
   She is going to buy a new bicycle.

El imperativo / The Imperative

The **imperative** form of a verb is the form used to give commands or directions.

Example: ¡Mira el perro ese!.............Look at that dog!

To form the imperative, drop the final **o** of the first-person present form and add the endings as shown in the chart.

	-ar verbs (saltar)	**-er verbs** (comer)	**-ir verbs** (escribir)
tú	salt<u>a</u>	com<u>e</u>	escrib<u>e</u>
Ud.	salt<u>e</u>	com<u>a</u>	escrib<u>a</u>
nosotros	salt<u>emos</u>	com<u>amos</u>	escrib<u>amos</u>
Uds.	salt<u>en</u>	com<u>an</u>	escrib<u>an</u>

These same endings are also applied to many irregular verbs.

The nosotros form is like the English "Let's . . ."

Example: ¡Comamos! ....Let's eat!

Escriba las órdenes en español.

saltar (tú) _____
jump

comer (tú) _____
eat

escuchar (Uds.) _____
listen

partir (Uds.) _____
leave

hablar español (tú) _____
speak Spanish

leer (nosotros) _____
read

mirar (nosotros) _____
look

escribir (Ud.) _____
write

El imperativo / The Imperative

Some verbs have irregular imperative forms. Here are the imperative forms for *ser* and *ir*.

	ser (to be)	ir (to go)
tú	sé	ve
Ud.	sea	vaya
nosotros	seamos	vayamos
Uds.	sean	vayan

Escriba las órdenes en español.

(tú)

Paint the fence! _____

Eat breakfast! _____

Drink the juice! (el jugo) _____

Be nice! _____

(ustedes)

Speak Spanish! _____

Look at the example! _____

Read page 50! _____

Describe the picture! _____

(nosotros)

Let's sing! _____

Let's watch TV! _____

Let's listen to music! _____

Let's go to a movie! _____

Repaso / Review

Escriba las oraciones en español.

1. _____

My dress is new.

2. _____

I am going to buy the black shoes.

3. _____

Do you want to go shopping?

4. _____

Wear the blue dress!

5. _____

How many sweaters do you have?

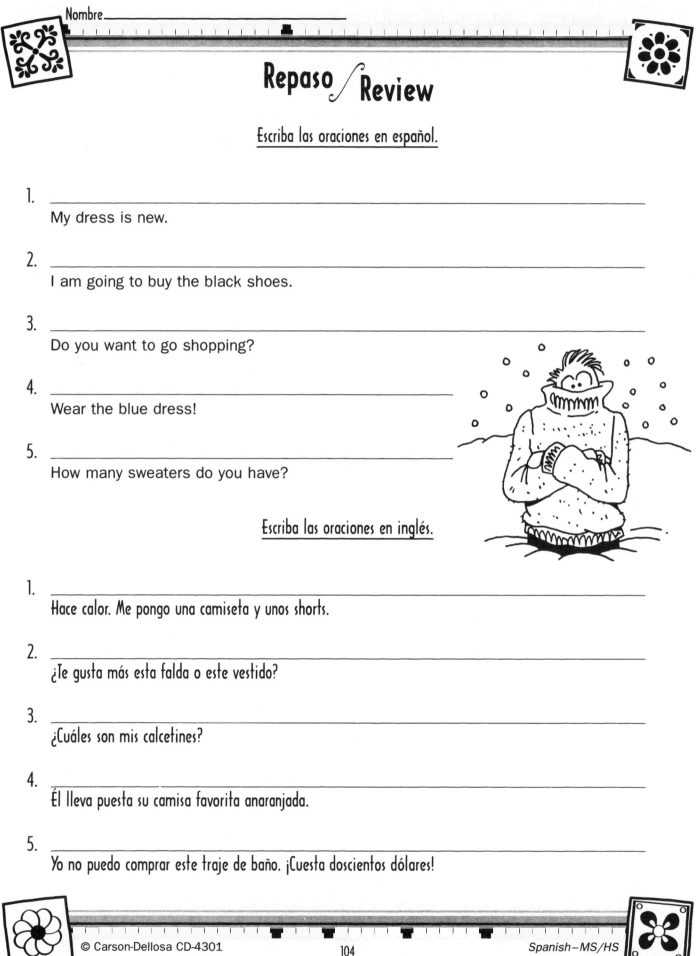

Escriba las oraciones en inglés.

1. _____

Hace calor. Me pongo una camiseta y unos shorts.

2. _____

¿Te gusta más esta falda o este vestido?

3. _____

¿Cuáles son mis calcetines?

4. _____

Él lleva puesta su camisa favorita anaranjada.

5. _____

Yo no puedo comprar este traje de baño. ¡Cuesta doscientos dólares!

Nombre_____

Crucigrama de repaso / Review Crossword

Across

2. lunes, martes, _____
4. ayer, _____, mañana
5. 17
9. ¿_____? Es la una.
11. third
13. _____, agosto, septiembre
15. ¿_____ cuesta el CD?
17. Me _____ la pijama antes de dormir.
18. Yo _____ de Argentina.
19. ¿_____ su nombre? = Do you know her name?

Down

1. Él _____ (can) hablar español e inglés.
3. ¿Tú _____ al fútbol?
4. to be hungry = tener _____
6. to read
7. Un _____ trabaja en la granja.
8. Carlos _____ España.
10. ¿Hablas español? Sí, yo _____ español.
11. Yo _____ 16 años.
12. Una jirafa es _____ alta que la niña.
14. Él _____ el clarinete.
16. ¿Cómo _____ llamas?

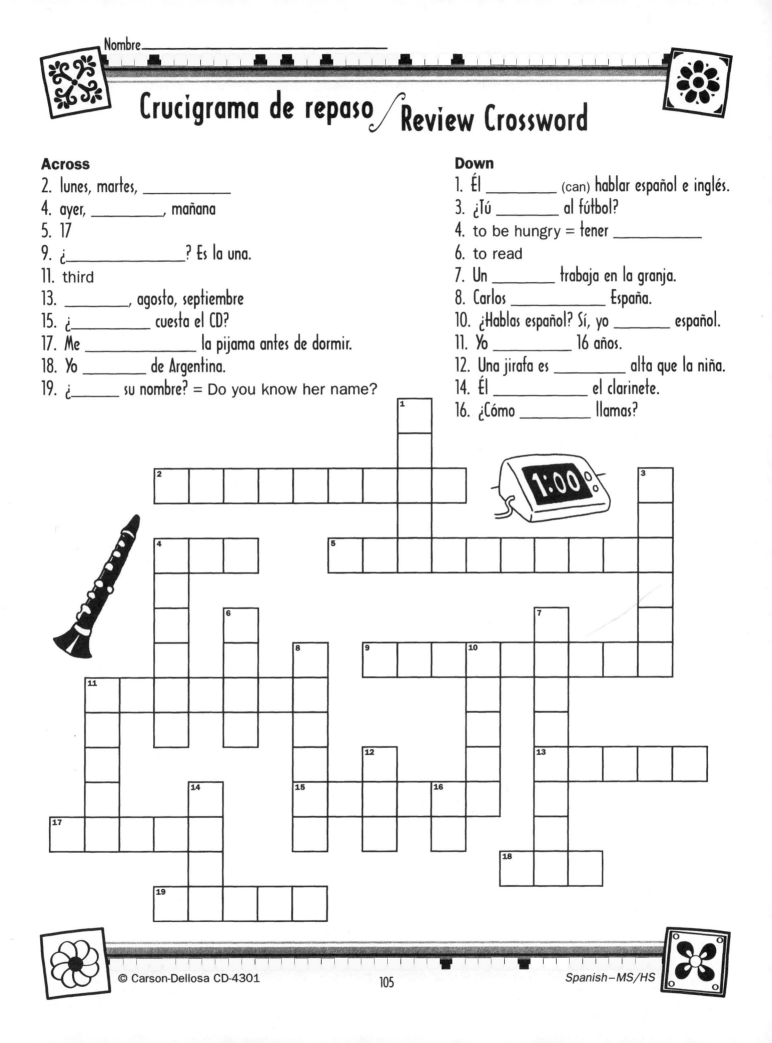

Vocabulario / Vocabulary

Vocabulary is listed alphabetically. Additional word lists appear at the end of page 112.

▸A

a (prep)	to; at
abrir (v)	to open
abuelo/-la (n) *m/f*	grandfather/grandmother
aburrido/-da (adj)	bored
aceituna (n) *f*	olive
adjetivo (n) *m*	adjective
aeropuerto (n) *m*	airport
agua (n) *f [m. in sing.]*	water
alfabeto (n) *m*	alphabet
alfombra (n) *f*	rug
alguien (pron)	someone
almuerzo (n) *m*	lunch
altavoz (n) *m*	loudspeaker
alto/-ta (adj)	tall
amable (adj)	nice
amarillo/-lla (adj)	yellow
amigo/-ga (n) *m/f*	friend
anaranjado/-da (adj)	orange
andar (v) **a**	to ride (a horse)
animal (n) *m*	animal
antes (adv)	before
año (n) *m*	year
aprender (v)	to learn
apropiado/-da (adj)	appropriate/suitable
aquí (adv)	here
araña (n) *f*	spider
árbol (n) *m*	tree
arreglar (v)	to fix or repair
arte (n) *m*	art
artículo (n) *m*	article
artista (n) *m/f*	artist
asustado/-da (adj)	scared
Australia (n) *f*	Australia
autobús (n) *m*	bus
autor/-ra (n) *m/f*	author
avión (n) *m*	airplane
ayer (adv)	yesterday
ayuda (n) *f*	help
azul (adj)	blue

▸B

bailar (v)	to dance
ballena (n) *f*	whale
banco (n) *m*	bank
bandera (n) *f*	flag

bañera (n) *f*	bathtub
baño (n) *m*	bathroom
barco (n) *m*	boat
barrer (v)	to sweep
basura (n) *f*	garbage, trash
batalla (n) *f*	battle
bebé (n) *m*	baby
beber (v)	to drink
béisbol (n) *m*	baseball
biblioteca (n) *f*	library
bicicleta (n) *f*	bicycle
bien (adv)	well
blanco/-ca (adj)	white
blusa (n) *f*	woman's shirt
boca (n) *f*	mouth
bolígrafo (n) *m*	pen
bombero (n) *m*	firefighter
bonito/-ta (adj)	pretty
borrador (n) *m*	eraser
borrego (n) *m*	sheep
Brasil (n) *m*	Brazil
brazo (n) *m*	arm
brillante (adj)	brilliant
bueno/-a (adj)	good
búho (n) *m*	owl

▸C

caballo (n) *m*	horse
cabeza (n) *f*	head
café (n) *m*	coffee
café (adj)	brown
cafetería (n) *f*	cafeteria
caja (n) *f*	box
calabaza (n) *f*	pumpkin
calcetín (n) *m*	sock
calculadora (n) *f*	calculator
calendario (n) *m*	calendar
calle (n) *f*	street
calor (n) *m*	heat
cama (n) *f*	bed
camarero/-ra (n) *m/f*	waiter/waitress
caminar (v)	to walk
camisa (n) *f*	man's shirt
camiseta (n) *f*	T-shirt
Canadá (n) *m*	Canada
cansado/-da (adj)	tired
cantar (v)	to sing

Vocabulario / Vocabulary

capital (n) *m*	capital	**corbata** (n) *f*	tie
carne (n) *m*	meat	**correo** (n) *m*	post office
carro (n) *m*	car	**correr** (v)	to run
carta (n) *f*	letter	**cortar** (v)	to cut
cartelera (n) *f*	bulletin board	**costar** (v)	to cost
cartero (n) *m*	mail carrier	**crayón** (n) *m*	crayon
casa (n) *f*	house	**creer** (v)	to believe
casado/-da (adj)	married	**crucero** (n) *m*	cruiser
castor (n) *m*	beaver	**crucigrama** (n) *f*	crossword puzzle
católico/-ca (adj)	Catholic	**cuarto** (n) *m*	quarter; room
cebolla (n) *f*	onion	**cuchara** (n) *f*	spoon
cena (n) *f*	dinner	**cuchillo** (n) *m*	knife
cepillo (n) *m*	brush	**cuello** (n) *m*	neck
cerca (n) *f*	fence	**culdado** (n) *m*	attention; care
cereza (n) *f*	cherry	**cuidar** (v)	to take care of
césped (n) *m*	lawn, grass	**cultivar** (v)	to grow
chaleco (n) *m*	vest	**cumpleaños** (n) *mpl*	birthday
chaqueta (n) *f*	jacket	**curioso/-sa** (adj)	curious
Chile (n) *m*	Chile		
chocolate (n) *m*	chocolate	▸D	
chofer/-ra (n) *m/f*	chauffeur		
cielo (n) *m*	sky	**dar** (v)	to give
ciencia (n) *f*	science	**deber** (v)	to owe
cine (n) *m*	movie theater	**decidir** (v)	to decide
cinta (n) *f*	tape	**decir** (v)	to say or tell
ciudad (n) *f*	city	**dedo de la mano** (n) *f*	finger
clase (n) *f*	class	**dedo del pie** (n) *m*	toe
clima (n) *f*	climate	**delfín** (n) *m*	dolphin
cocina (n) *f*	kitchen	**dentista** (n) *m/f*	dentist
cocinar (v)	to cook	**deporte** (n) *m*	sport
cocinero/-ra (n) *m/f*	cook	**desayuno** (n) *m*	breakfast
coco (n) *m*	coconut	**describir** (v)	to describe
collar (n) *m*	necklace	**después** (adv)	after
color (n) *m*	color	**día** (n) *m*	day
comedor (n) *m*	dining room	**dibujo** (n) *m*	picture
comer (v)	to eat	**dibujo animado** (n) *m*	cartoon
comlda (n) *f*	food	**diente** (n) *m*	tooth
cómoda (n) *f*	dresser	**dinero** (n) *m*	money
completar (v)	to complete or finish	**dirección** (n) *f*	address
completo/-ta (adj)	complete	**disco compacto** (n) *m*	CD
compra (n) *f*	purchase	**doctor/-ra** (n) *m/f*	doctor
comprar (v)	to buy	**dólar** (n) *m*	dollar
computadora (n) *f*	computer	**dolor** (n) *m*	pain
conclusión (n) *f*	conclusion	**ducha** (n) *f*	shower
conejo (n) *m*	rabbit	**dulce** (adj)	sweet
conocer (v)	to know, be familiar with		
contar (v)	to count	▸E	
contento/-ta (adj)	happy; content		
contestar (v)	to answer	**educación física** (n) *f*	physical education
conversación (n) *f*	conversation	**ejemplo** (n) *m*	example
		elefante (n) *m*	elephant
		empezar (v)	to begin

 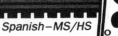

Vocabulario / Vocabulary

empleado/-da (n) *m/f*	employee
encontrar (v)	to find
enfermero/-ra (n) *m/f*	nurse
enfermo/-ma (adj)	sick or ill
enojado/-da (adj)	angry
entrevista (n) *f*	interview
enviar (v)	to send
equipo (n) *m*	team
escalador (n) *m*	climber (one who climbs)
escarabajo (n) *m*	beetle
escribir (v)	to write
escuchar (v)	to listen (to)
escuela (n) *f*	school
ese/esa (adj)	that, those
España (n) *f*	Spain
español/-la (adj)	Spanish
espejo (n) *m*	mirror
esposo/-sa (n) *m/f*	spouse (husband/wife)
esquina (n) *f*	corner
estación (n) *f*	season
estación de bomberos (n) *f*	fire station
Estados Unidos (n) *mpl*	the United States
estadounidense (adj)	American
estar (v)	to be
este/-ta (adj)	this/these
estéreo (n) *m*	stereo
estropeado/-da (adj)	broken
estudiante (n) *m/f*	student
estudiar (v)	to study
estudios sociales (n) *mpl*	social studies
estufa (n) *f*	stove
éxito (n) *m*	success

▸F

falda (n) *f*	skirt
favorito/-ta (adj)	favorite
fecha (n) *f*	date
feliz (adj)	happy
feo/fea (adj)	ugly
fiesta (n) *f*	party
flamenco (n) *m*	flamingo
flor (n) *f*	flower
forma (n) *f*	form
fracción (n) *f*	fraction
frambuesa (n) *f*	raspberry
frase (n) *f*	phrase
fresa (n) *f*	strawberry
fresco (n) *m*	fresh air; coolness
frío (n) *m*	cold

frito (adj)	fried
fruta (n) *f*	fruit
fuego (n) *m*	fire
fuerte (adj)	loud
fumar (v)	to smoke
fútbol (n) *m*	soccer

▸G

gabinete (n) *m*	cabinet
galleta (n) *f*	cookie
ganar (v)	to win
garaje (n) *m*	garage
gastar (v)	to spend
gato (n) *m*	cat
gerundio (n) *m*	gerund
gigante (n) *m*	giant
gigante (adj)	giant, huge
golf (n) *m*	golf
grande (adj)	big; old
granja (n) *f*	farm
granjero/a (n) *m/f*	farmer
grapadora (n) *f*	stapler
gritar (v)	to scream
guapo/-pa (adj)	good-looking, attractive
guisante (n) *m*	pea
guitarra (n) *f*	guitar

▸H

hablar (v)	to speak or talk
hacer (v)	to make or do
hambre (n) *f [m. in sing.]*	hunger
hamburguesa (n) *f*	hamburger
helado (n) *m*	ice cream
hermano/-na (n) *m/f*	brother/sister
herramienta (n) *f*	tool
hindú (adj)	Hindu
historia (n) *f*	history
hoja (n) *f*	leaf
hombre (n) *m*	man
hombre de negocios (n) *m*	businessman
hora (n) *f*	hour
hormiga (n) *f*	ant
horno (n) *m*	oven
hospital (n) *m*	hospital
hotel (n) *m*	hotel
hoy (adv)	today
hueso (n) *m*	bone
huevo (n) *m*	egg

Vocabulario / Vocabulary

▸I

idioma (n) *m*	language
iglesia (n) *f*	church
iguana (n) *f*	iguana
importante (adj)	important
inglés/-sa (adj)	English
instrumento (n) *m*	instrument
inteligente (adj)	intelligent
interesante (adj)	interesting
invierno (n) *m*	winter
ir (v)	to go
isla (n) *f*	island

▸J

Japón	Japan
jirafa (n) *f*	giraffe
joven (adj)	young
jugar (v)	to play (a sport or game)
jugo (n) *m*	juice

▸K

Kenia (n) *f*	Kenya
koala (n) *f*	koala

▸L

ladrar (v)	to bark
lámpara (n) *f*	lamp
lancha (n) *f*	motorboat
lápiz (n) *m*	pencil
largo/-ga (adj)	long
lavamanos (n) *m*	bathroom sink
lavar (v)	to wash
lección (n) *f*	lesson
leche (n) *f*	milk
lectura (n) *f*	reading
leer (v)	to read
lejos (adv)	far
león (n) *m*	lion
letra (n) *f*	letter
libertad (n) *f*	liberty
libro (n) *m*	book
limón (n) *m*	lemon or lime
limpiar (v)	to clean
listo/-ta (adj)	ready
llamar (v)	to call
llamarse (v)	to be called, to be named
llanta (n) *f*	tire
llave (n) *f*	key

llevar (v)	to wear
llorar (v)	to cry
llover (v)	to rain
lombriz (n) *f*	earthworm
lotería (n) *f*	lottery
lumbre (n) *f*	fire (in fireplace)
luna (n) *f*	moon
luz (n) *f*	(overhead) light

▸M

madre (n) *f*	mother
maduro/-ra (adj)	ripe
maestro/-tra (n) *m/f*	teacher
mal (adv)	not well, badly
malo/-la (adj)	bad
manejar (v)	to drive
mano (n) *f*	hand
mantel (n) *m*	tablecloth
manzana (n) *f*	apple
mañana (n) *f*	morning
mañana (adv)	tomorrow
mapa (n) *m*	map
más (adv)	more
matemáticas (n) *fpl*	mathematics
maternidad (n) *f*	maternity
mayor (adj)	older
mecánico/a (n) *m/f*	mechanic
medio/-dia (adj)	half
mediodía (n) *f*	noon
mejor (adj/adv)	better
menor (adj)	younger
menos (adv)	less
mercado (n) *m*	market
merienda (n) *f*	snack
mes (n) *m*	month
mesa (n) *f*	table
mexicano/-na (adj)	Mexican
México (n) *m*	Mexico
miedo (n) *m*	fear
mientras (conj)	while
mirar (v)	to watch or look at
monstruo (n) *m*	monster
montar (v)	to ride (as a horse)
morado/-da (adj)	purple
mucho/-cha (adj)	much, many; a lot of
mujer (n) *f*	woman
museo (n) *m*	museum
música (n) *f*	music

Vocabulario / Vocabulary

►N

nación (n) *f*	nation
nadar (v)	to swim
naranja (n) *f*	orange
nariz (n) *f*	nose
negativo/-va (adj)	negative
negro/-gra (adj)	black
nervioso/-sa (adj)	nervous
nevar (v)	to snow
niebla (n) *f*	fog
nieve (n) *f*	snow
niño/-ña (n) *m/f*	child (boy/girl)
no (adv)	no
noche (n) *f*	night
nombre (n) *m*	name
nota (n) *f*	grade (A, B, . . .)
novia (n) *f*	girlfriend
nube (n) *f*	cloud
nuevo/-va (adj)	new
número (n) *m*	number

►Ñ

ñu (n) *m*	gnu

►O

oficina (n) *f*	office
ojo (n) *m*	eye
ola (n) *f*	wave
oración (n) *f*	sentence
oreja (n) *f*	ear
oro (n) *m*	gold
oscuridad (n) *f*	dark
otoño (n) *m*	autumn

►P

padre (n) *m*	father
página (n) *f*	page
pájaro (n) *m*	bird
palabra (n) *f*	word
pan (n) *m*	bread
pantalones (n) *mpl*	pants
papa (n) *f*	potato
papalote (n) *m*	kite
papel (n) *m*	paper
papelera (n) *f*	wastepaper basket
pared (n) *f*	wall
parque (n) *m*	park
partir (v)	to leave

pasear (v)	to take for a walk or ride
pasta (n) *f*	pasta
pastel (n) *m*	cake
pasto (n) *m*	grass; pasture
pegamento (n) *m*	glue
película (n) *f*	film, movie
pelo (n) *m*	hair
pelota (n) *f*	ball
pensar (v)	to think
peor (adj/adv)	worse
pepino (n) *m*	cucumber
pequeño/-ña (adj)	small, young
perfumar (v)	to perfume, to fill with scent
pero (conj)	but
perro (n) *m*	dog
persona (n) *f*	person
personalidad (n) *f*	personality
pescado (n) *m*	fish
piano (n) *m*	piano
pierna (n) *f*	leg
pijama (n) *f*	pajamas
pimentero (n) *m*	pepper shaker
pimiento (n) *m*	pepper
pincel (n) *m*	paintbrush
pintar (v)	to paint
pintura (n) *f*	paint
piso (n) *m*	floor
pizarrón (n) *m*	chalkboard
planeta (n) *m*	planet
planta (n) *f*	plant
plátano (n) *m*	banana
platillo (n) *m*	saucer
plato (n) *m*	plate
playa (n) *f*	beach
pluma (n) *f*	feather
poco/-ca (adj)	little (qty), few
poco (adv)	not much
poder (v)	to be able to, can
poema (n) *m*	poem
pollo (n) *m*	chicken
ponerse (v)	to put on
posesión (n) *f*	possession
posible (adj)	possible
práctica (n) *f*	practice
practicar (v)	to practice
pregunta (n) *f*	question
preguntar (v)	to ask
preposición (n) *f*	preposition
presentación (n) *f*	introduction; presentation
presentar (v)	to introduce

110 *Spanish–MS/HS*

Vocabulario / Vocabulary

presidente (n) *m* — president
primavera (n) *f* — spring
primo/-ma (n) *m/f* — cousin
problema (n) *m* — problem
profesor/-ra (n) *m/f* — professor
programa (n) *m* — program
pronombre (n) *m* — pronoun
próximo/-ma (adj) — next
puerco (n) *m* — pig
puerta (n) *f* — door
punto (n) *m* — dot
pupitre (n) *m* — desk

▸Q

querer (v) — to want
queso (n) *m* — cheese

▸R

rábano (n) *m* — radish
radio (n) *f* — radio
rama (n) *f* — branch
rápido (adv) — fast, quickly
rastrillar (v) — to rake
rata (n) *f* — rat
ratón (n) *m* — mouse
razón (n) *f* — reason; truth
recámara (n) *f* — bedroom
recibir (v) — to receive
recuerdo (n) *m* — souvenir
refrigerador (n) *m* — refrigerator
regalo (n) *m* — gift, present
regla (n) *f* — ruler
reloj (n) *m* — clock
repartir (v) — to deliver
repaso (n) *m* — review
reseña (n) *f* — report
respuesta (n) *f* — answer (to a question)
restaurante (n) *m* — restaurant
revista (n) *f* — magazine
rival (n) *m/f* — rival; opponent
rizado/-da (adj) — curly
roca (n) *f* — rock
rojo/-ja (adj) — red
ropero (n) *m* — closet
rosado/-da (adj) — pink
Rusia (n) *f* — Russia

▸S

saber (v) — to know
sacapuntas (n) *m* — pencil sharpener

sacar (v) — to take out
sala (n) *f* — living room
salero (n) *m* — salt shaker
salir (v) — to leave
saltamontes (n) *m* — grasshopper
saltar (v) — to jump
salud (n) *f* — health
sandía (n) *f* — watermelon
sándwich (n) *m* — sandwich
sed (n) *f* — thirst
segadora (n) *f* — lawn mower
semana (n) *f* — week
ser (v) — to be
serio/-ria (adj) — serious
servilleta (n) *f* — napkin
si (conj) — if
sí (adv) — yes
siempre (adv) — always
shorts (n) *mpl* — shorts
siguiente (adj) — following
silla (n) *f* — chair
simpático/-ca (adj) — kind
sin (prep) — without
sistema (n) *m* — system
sofá (n) *m* — sofa or couch
sol (n) *m* — sun
sombrero (n) *m* — hat
sopa (n) *f* — soup
sordo/-da (adj) — deaf
sueño (n) *m* — sleep
suerte (n) *f* — fortune; luck
suéter (n) *m* — sweater
sujeto (n) *m* — subject
supermercado (n) *m* — supermarket

▸T

taller (n) *m* — workshop or garage
también (adv) — too, also, as well
tambor (n) *m* — drum
tarde (n) *f* — afternoon
tarea (n) *f* — homework
taza (n) *f* — cup
tazón (n) *m* — bowl
teléfono (n) *m* — telephone
telegrama (n) *m* — telegram
televisión (n) *f* — television
tema (n) *m* — theme
tenedor (n) *m* — fork
tener (v) — to have
tenis (n) *m* — tennis

Vocabulario / Vocabulary

terminar (v)	to end		
tiempo (n) *m*	weather		
tienda (n) *f*	store		
tigre (n) *m*	tiger		
tijeras (n) *fpl*	scissors		
tío/tía (n) *m/f*	uncle/aunt		
tiza (n) *f*	chalk		
tocar (v)	to play (an instrument)		
tomar (v)	to take		
tomate (n) *m*	tomato		
trabajador/-ra (adj)	hard-working		
traje (n) *m*	suit		
traje de baño (n) *m*	swimsuit		
transatlántico (n) *m*	ocean liner		
trazar (v)	to draw; to trace		
trepar (v)	to climb		
triste (adj)	sad		
trompeta (n) *f*	trumpet		

►U

uniforme (n) *m*	uniform
universidad (n) *f*	university or college
uva (n) *f*	grape

►V

vaca (n) *f*	cow
vacación (n) *f*	vacation
vaso (n) *m*	glass
vecino (n) *m*	neighbor
vegetal (n) *m*	vegetable
velero (n) *m*	sailboat
venado (n) *m*	deer
vender (v)	to sell
ventana (n) *f*	window
ver (v)	to see
verano (n) *m*	summer
verbo (n) *m*	verb
verde (adj)	green
vestido (n) *m*	dress
viajar (v)	to travel
video (n) *m*	video tape
viejo/-ja (adj)	old
viento (n) *m*	wind
violín (n) *m*	violin
visitar (v)	to visit
vivir (v)	to write
volar (v)	to fly
voleibol (n) *m*	volleyball

►W

wafle (n) *m*	waffle

►X

xilófono (n) *m*	xylophone

►Y

yate (n) *m*	yacht

►Z

zapato (n) *m*	shoe
zorro (n) *m*	fox

►Additional Word Lists

lunes	Monday
martes	Tuesday
miércoles	Wednesday
jueves	Thursday
viernes	Friday
sábado	Saturday
domingo	Sunday
enero	January
febrero	February
marzo	March
abril	April
mayo	May
junio	June
julio	July
agosto	August
septiembre	September
octubre	October
noviembre	November
diciembre	December
a qué hora	at what time
cómo	how
cuál	which
cuándo	when
cuánto	how much
dónde	where
por qué	why
qué	what
quién	who

Answer Key

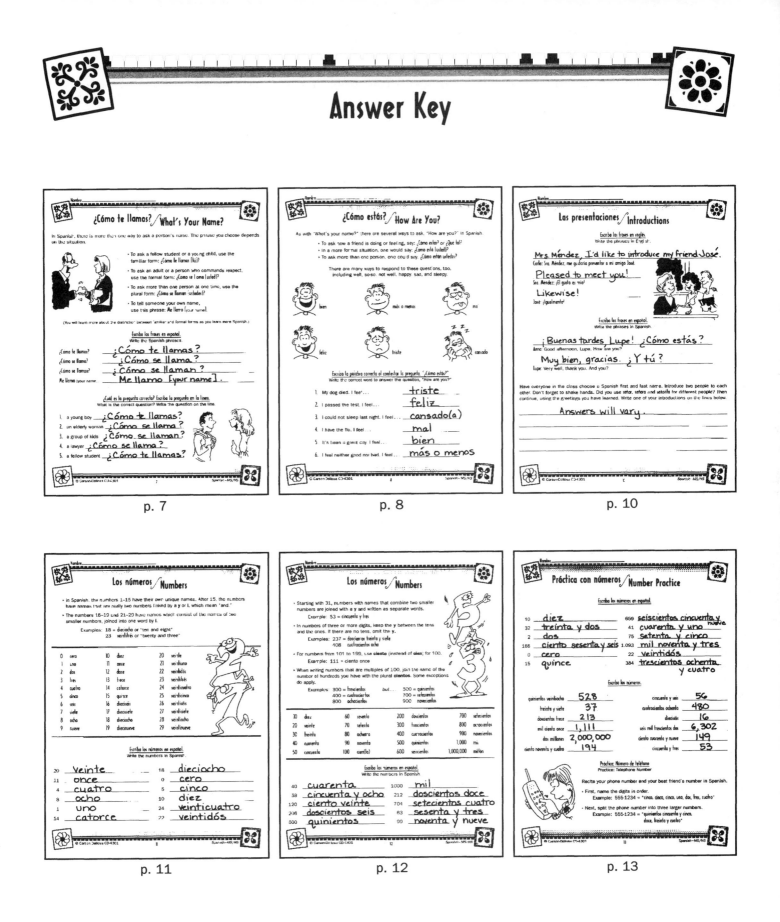

p. 7

p. 8

p. 10

p. 11

p. 12

p. 13

Answer Key

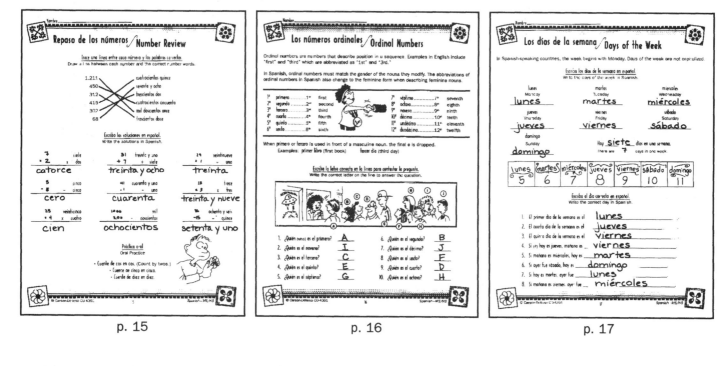

p. 15

p. 16

p. 17

p. 18

p. 19

p. 20

Answer Key

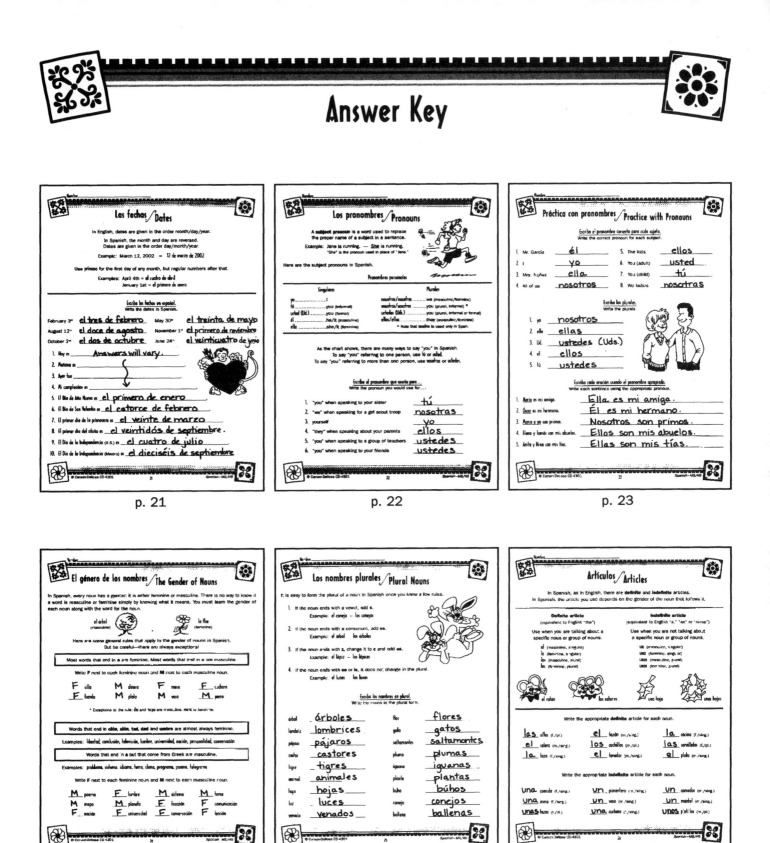

p. 21

Las fechas / Dates

In English, dates are given in the order month/day/year.
In Spanish, the month and day are reversed.
Dates are given in the order day/month/year.

Example: March 12, 2002 = 12 de marzo de 2002

Use *primero* for the first day of any month, but regular numbers after that.

Examples: April 4th = el cuatro de abril
January 1st = el primero de enero

Escriba las fechas en español.
Write the dates in Spanish.

February 3rd — **el tres de febrero**   May 30th — **el treinta de mayo**
August 12th — **el doce de agosto**   November 1st — **el primero de noviembre**
October 2nd — **el dos de octubre**   June 24th — **el veinticuatro de junio**

1. Hoy es — **Answers will vary.**
2. Mañana es —
3. Ayer fue —
4. Mi cumpleaños es —
5. El Día de Año Nuevo es — **el primero de enero**
6. El Día de San Valentín es — **el catorce de febrero**
7. El primer día de la primavera es — **el veinte de marzo**
8. El primer día del otoño es — **el veintidós de septiembre**.
9. El Día de la Independencia (U.S.) es — **el cuatro de julio**
10. El Día de la Independencia (Mexico) es — **el dieciséis de septiembre**

Los pronombres / Pronouns

A **subject pronoun** is a word used to replace the proper name of a subject in a sentence.

Example: Jane is running. — She is running.
"She" is the pronoun used in place of "Jane."

Here are the subject pronouns in Spanish.

Pronombres personales

Singulares		Plurales	
yo	I	nosotros/nosotras	we (masculine/feminine)
tú	you (informal)	vosotros/vosotras	you (plural, informal) *
usted (Ud.)	you (formal)	ustedes (Uds.)	you (plural, informal or formal)
él	he/it (masculine)	ellos/ellas	they (masculine/feminine)
ella	she/it (feminine)		

* Note that *vosotros* is used only in Spain.

As the chart shows, there are many ways to say "you" in Spanish.
To say "you" referring to one person, use *tú* or *usted.*
To say "you" referring to more than one person, use *vosotros* or *ustedes.*

Escriba el pronombre que usaría para...
Write the pronoun you would use for...

1. "you" when speaking to your sister — **tú**
2. "we" when speaking for a girl scout troop — **nosotras**
3. yourself — **yo**
4. "they" when speaking about your parents — **ellos**
5. "you" when speaking to a group of teachers — **ustedes**
6. "you" when speaking to your friends — **ustedes**

p. 22

Práctica con pronombres / Practice with Pronouns

Escriba el pronombre correcto para cada sujeto.
Write the correct pronoun for each subject.

1. Mr. García — **él**   5. The kids — **ellos**
2. I — **yo**   6. You (adult) — **usted**
3. Mrs. Núñez — **ella**   7. You (child) — **tú**
4. All of us — **nosotros**   8. We ladies — **nosotras**

Escriba los plurales.
Write the plurals.

1. yo — **nosotros**
2. ella — **ellas**
3. Ud. — **ustedes (Uds.)**
4. el — **ellos**
5. tú — **ustedes**

Escriba cada oración usando el pronombre apropiado.
Write each sentence using the appropriate pronoun.

1. María es mi amiga. — **Ella es mi amiga.**
2. Óscar es mi hermano. — **Él es mi hermano.**
3. Marco y yo son primos. — **Nosotros son primos.**
4. Elena y Tomás son mis abuelos. — **Ellos son mis abuelos.**
5. Anita y Nina son mis tías. — **Ellas son mis tías.**

p. 23

El género de los nombres / The Gender of Nouns

In Spanish, every noun has a gender; it is either feminine or masculine. There is no way to know if a word is masculine or feminine simply by knowing what it means. But you must learn the gender of each noun along with the word for the noun.

el árbol (masculine)   la flor (feminine)

Here are some general rules that apply to the gender of nouns in Spanish.
But be careful—there are always exceptions!

Most words that end in **a** are feminine. Most words that end in **o** are masculine.

Write **F** next to each feminine noun and **M** next to each masculine noun.

F silla   **M** dinero   **F** mesa   **F** cuchara
F tienda   **M** plato   **M** vaso   **M** perro

* Exceptions to the rule: *día* and *mapa* are masculine; *mano* is feminine.

Words that end in **ción, sión, tad, dad** and **umbre** are almost always feminine.

Examples: libertad, conclusión, televisión, lumbre, universidad, nación, personalidad, conversación

Words that end in **a** but that come from Greek are masculine.

Examples: problema, sistema, tema, clima, programa, poema, telegrama

Write **F** next to each feminine noun and **M** next to each masculine noun.

M poema   **F** lumbre   **M** sistema   **M** tema
M mapa   **M** planeta   **F** fracción   **F** comunicación
F nación   **F** universidad   **F** conversación   **F** lección

p. 24

Los nombres plurales / Plural Nouns

It is easy to form the plural of a noun in Spanish once you know a few rules.

1. If the noun ends in a vowel, add s.
   Example: el conejo – los conejos

2. If the noun ends with a consonant, add es.
   Example: el árbol – los árboles

3. If the noun ends with z, change it to c and add es.
   Example: el lápiz – los lápices

4. If the noun ends in es or is, it does not change in the plural.
   Example: el lunes – los lunes

Escriba los nombres en plural.
Write the nouns in the plural form.

árbol — **árboles**   flor — **flores**
lombriz — **lombrices**   gato — **gatos**
pájaro — **pájaros**   saltamontes — **saltamontes**
castor — **castores**   pluma — **plumas**
tigre — **tigres**   iguana — **iguanas**
animal — **animales**   planta — **plantas**
hoja — **hojas**   búho — **búhos**
luz — **luces**   conejo — **conejos**
venado — **venados**   ballena — **ballenas**

p. 25

Artículos / Articles

In Spanish, as in English, there are **definite** and **indefinite** articles.
In Spanish, the article you use depends on the gender of the noun that follows it.

Definite article
(equivalent to English "the")

Use when you are talking about a specific noun or group of nouns.

el (masculine, singular)
la (feminine, singular)
los (masculine, plural)
las (feminine, plural)

Indefinite article
(equivalent to English "a," "an" or "some")

Use when you are not talking about a specific noun or group of nouns.

un (masculine, singular)
una (feminine, singular)
unos (masculine, plural)
unas (feminine, plural)

el ratón   los ratones   una hoja   unas hojas

Write the appropriate **definite** article for each noun.

las sillas (f./pl.)   **el** tazón (m./sing.)   **la** cocina (f./sing.)
el salero (m./sing.)   **los** cuchillos (m./pl.)   **las** servilletas (f./pl.)
la taza (f./sing.)   **el** tenedor (m./sing.)   **el** plato (m./sing.)

Write the appropriate **indefinite** article for each noun.

una comida (f./sing.)   **un** pimentero (m./sing.)   **un** comedor (m./sing.)
una mesa (f./sing.)   **un** vaso (m./sing.)   **un** mantel (m./sing.)
unas tazas (f./pl.)   **una** cuchara (f./sing.)   **unos** platillos (m./pl.)

p. 26

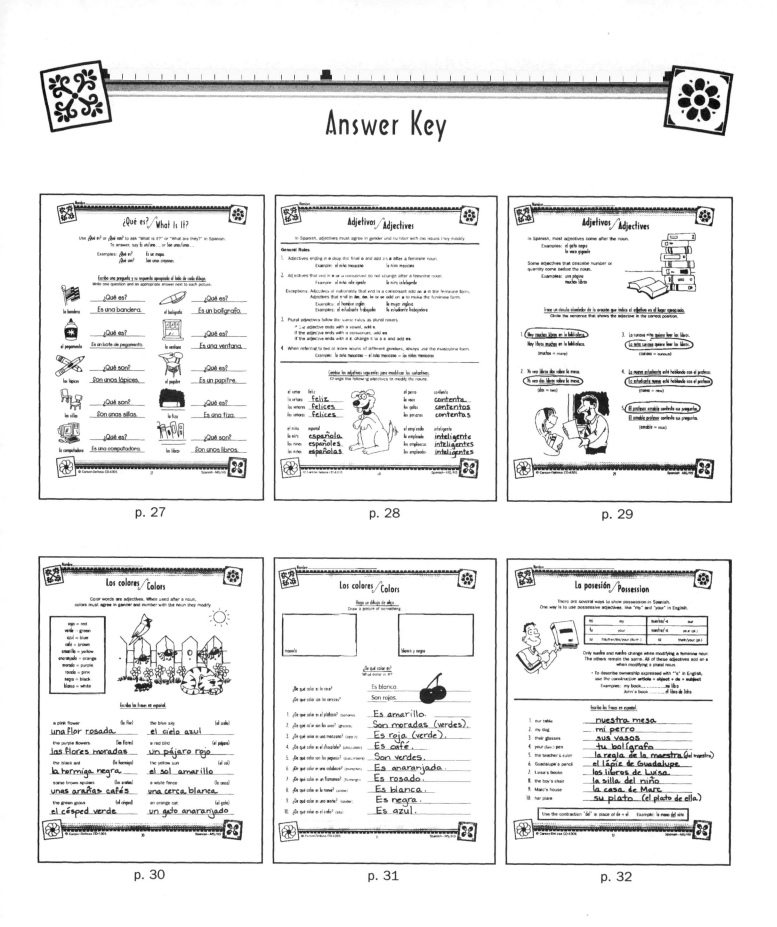

p. 27

p. 28

p. 29

p. 30

p. 31

p. 32

Answer Key

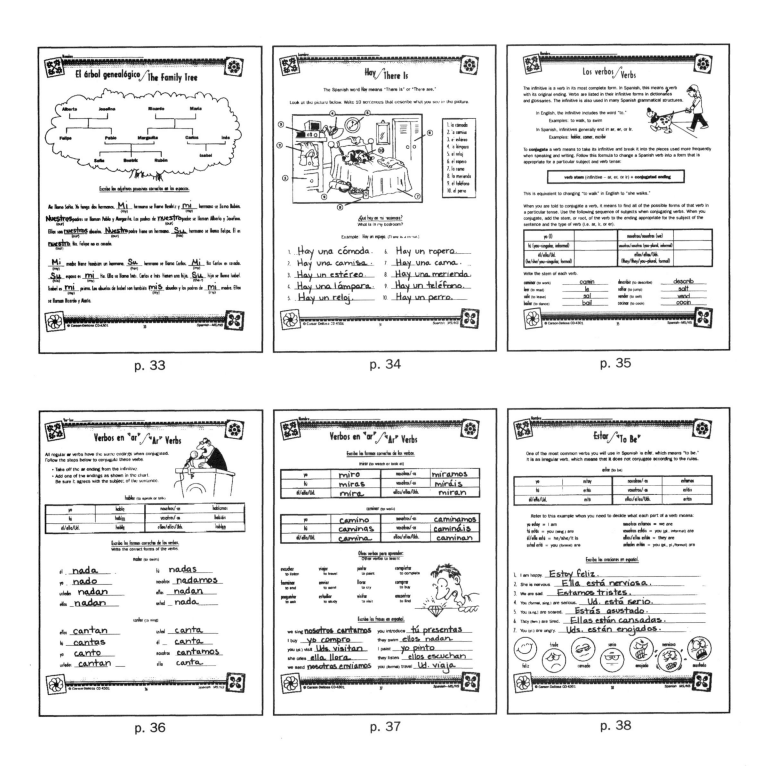

p. 33

p. 34

p. 35

p. 36

p. 37

p. 38

Answer Key

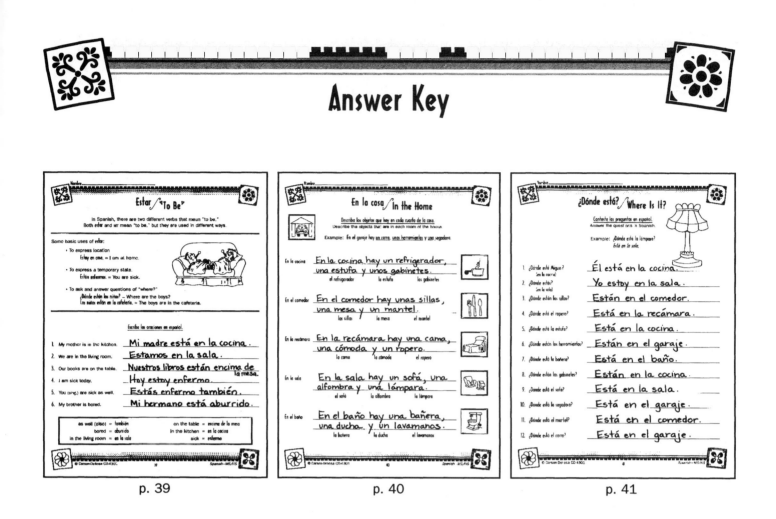

p. 39

Estar / "To Be"

In Spanish, there are two different verbs that mean "to be."
Both *estar* and *ser* mean "to be," but they are used in different ways.

Some basic uses of *estar*:

- To express location
  Estoy en casa. = I am at home.

- To express a temporary state.
  Están enfermos. = You are sick.

- To ask and answer questions of "where?"
  ¿Dónde están los niños? – Where are the boys?
  Los niños están en la cafetería. = The boys are in the cafeteria.

Escribe las oraciones en español.

1. My mother is in the kitchen. **Mi madre está en la cocina.**
2. We are in the living room. **Estamos en la sala.**
3. Our books are on the table. **Nuestros libros están encima de la mesa.**
4. I am sick today. **Hoy estoy enfermo.**
5. You (sing.) are sick as well. **Estás enfermo también.**
6. My brother is bored. **Mi hermano está aburrido.**

as well (also) = también	on the table = encima de la mesa
bored = aburrido	in the kitchen = en la cocina
in the living room = en la sala	sick = enfermo

p. 40

En la casa / In the Home

Describe los objetos que hay en cada cuarto de la casa.
Describe the objects that are in each room of the house.

Example: En el garaje hay *un carro*, *unas herramientas* y *una segadora*.

En la cocina — **En la cocina hay un refrigerador, una estufa y unos gabinetes.**
el refrigerador   la estufa   los gabinetes

En el comedor — **En el comedor hay unas sillas, una mesa y un mantel.**
las sillas   la mesa   el mantel

En la recámara — **En la recámara hay una cama, una cómoda y un ropero.**
la cama   la cómoda   el ropero

En la sala — **En la sala hay un sofá, una alfombra y una lámpara.**
el sofá   la alfombra   la lámpara

En el baño — **En el baño hay una bañera, una ducha, y un lavamanos.**
la bañera   la ducha   el lavamanos

p. 41

¿Dónde está? / Where Is It?

Contesta las preguntas en español.
Answer the questions in Spanish.

Example: ¿Dónde está la lámpara?
Está en la sala.

1. ¿Dónde está Miguel? **Él está en la cocina.**
2. ¿Dónde estás? **Yo estoy en la sala.**
3. ¿Dónde están las sillas? **Están en el comedor.**
4. ¿Dónde está el ropero? **Está en la recámara.**
5. ¿Dónde está la estufa? **Está en la cocina.**
6. ¿Dónde están las herramientas? **Están en el garaje.**
7. ¿Dónde está la bañera? **Está en el baño.**
8. ¿Dónde están los gabinetes? **Están en la cocina.**
9. ¿Dónde está el sofá? **Está en la sala.**
10. ¿Dónde está la segadora? **Está en el garaje.**
11. ¿Dónde está el mantel? **Está en el comedor.**
12. ¿Dónde está el carro? **Está en el garaje.**

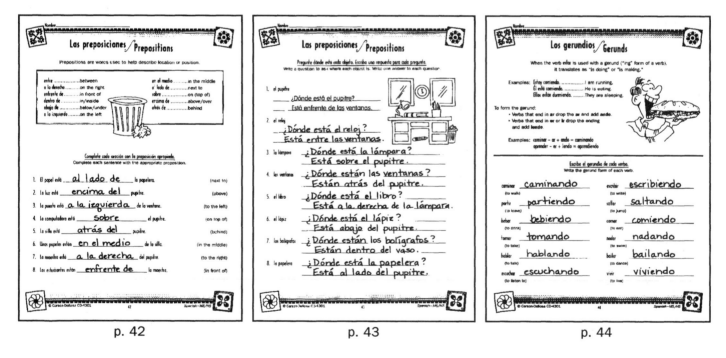

p. 42

Las preposiciones / Prepositions

Prepositions are words used to help describe location or position.

entre	between	en el medio	in the middle
a la derecha	on the right	al lado de	next to
enfrente de	in front of	sobre	on (top of)
dentro de	in/inside	encima de	above/over
abajo de	below/under	atrás de	behind
a la izquierda	on the left		

Complete cada oración con la preposición apropiada.
Complete each sentence with the appropriate preposition.

1. El papel está **al lado de** la papelera. (next to)
2. La luz está **encima del** pupitre. (above)
3. La puerta está **a la izquierda** de la ventana. (to the left)
4. La computadora está **sobre** el pupitre. (on top of)
5. La silla está **atrás del** pupitre. (behind)
6. Unos papeles están **en el medio** de la silla. (in the middle)
7. La maestra está **a la derecha** del pupitre. (to the right)
8. Los estudiantes están **enfrente de** la maestra. (in front of)

p. 43

Las preposiciones / Prepositions

Pregunta dónde está cada objeto. Escribe una respuesta para cada pregunta.
Write a question to ask where each object is. Write one answer to each question.

1. el pupitre
   ¿Dónde está el pupitre?
   Está enfrente de las ventanas.
2. el reloj
   ¿Dónde está el reloj?
   Está entre las ventanas.
3. la lámpara
   ¿Dónde está la lámpara?
   Está sobre el pupitre.
4. las ventanas
   ¿Dónde están las ventanas?
   Están atrás del pupitre.
5. el libro
   ¿Dónde está el libro?
   Está a la derecha de la lámpara.
6. el lápiz
   ¿Dónde está el lápiz?
   Está abajo del pupitre.
7. los bolígrafos
   ¿Dónde están los bolígrafos?
   Están dentro del vaso.
8. la papelera
   ¿Dónde está la papelera?
   Está al lado del pupitre.

p. 44

Los gerundios / Gerunds

When the verb *estar* is used with a gerund ("ing" form of a verb),
it translates as "is doing" or "is making."

Examples: *Estoy comiendo.* .... I am running.
Él está comiendo. .... He is eating.
Ellas están durmiendo. .... They are sleeping.

To form the gerund:
- Verbs that end in *ar* drop the *ar* and add *ando*.
- Verbs that end in *er* or *ir* drop the ending and add *iendo*.

Examples: caminar - *ar* + *ando* = caminando
aprender - *er* + *iendo* = aprendiendo

Escribe el gerundio de cada verbo.
Write the gerund form of each verb.

caminar (to walk)	**caminando**	escribir (to write)	**escribiendo**
partir (to leave)	**partiendo**	saltar (to jump)	**saltando**
beber (to drink)	**bebiendo**	comer (to eat)	**comiendo**
tomar (to take)	**tomando**	nadar (to swim)	**nadando**
hablar (to talk)	**hablando**	bailar (to dance)	**bailando**
escuchar (to listen to)	**escuchando**	vivir (to live)	**viviendo**

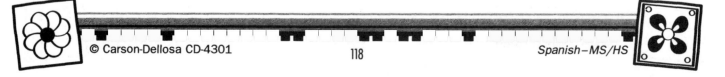

Answer Key

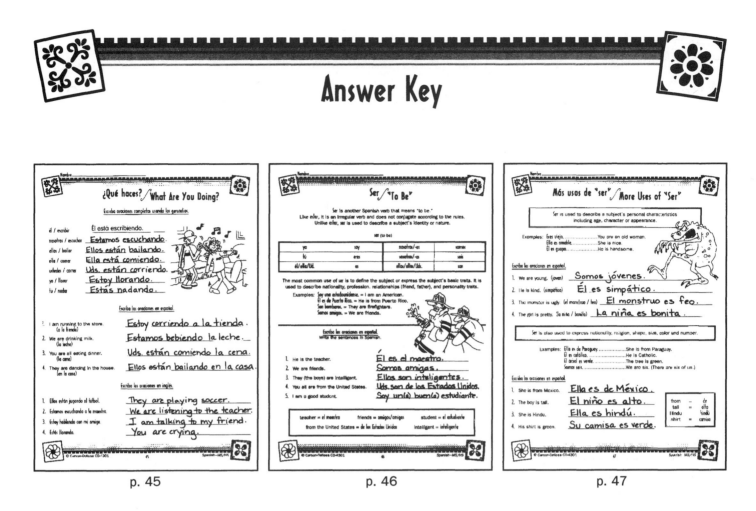

p. 45

¿Qué haces? / What Are You Doing?

Escriba oraciones completas usando los gerundios.

él / escribir	Él está escribiendo.
nosotras / escuchar	Estamos escuchando.
ellos / bailar	Ellos están bailando.
ella / comer	Ella está comiendo.
ustedes / correr	Uds. están corriendo.
yo / llorar	Estoy llorando.
tú / nadar	Estás nadando.

Escriba las oraciones en español.

1. I am running to the store. (a la tienda) — Estoy corriendo a la tienda.
2. We are drinking milk. (la leche) — Estamos bebiendo la leche.
3. You are all eating dinner. (la cena) — Uds. están comiendo la cena.
4. They are dancing in the house. (en la casa) — Ellos están bailando en la casa.

Escriba las oraciones en inglés.

1. Ellos están jugando al fútbol. — They are playing soccer.
2. Estamos escuchando a la maestra. — We are listening to the teacher.
3. Estoy hablando con mi amiga. — I am talking to my friend.
4. Estás llorando. — You are crying.

p. 46

Ser / "To Be"

Ser is another Spanish verb that means "to be."
Like estar, it is an irregular verb and does not conjugate according to the rules.
Unlike estar, ser is used to describe a subject's identity or nature.

ser (to be)			
yo	soy	nosotros/-as	somos
tú	eres	vosotros/-as	sois
él/ella/Ud.	es	ellos/ellas/Uds.	son

The most common use of ser is to define the subject or express the subject's basic traits. It is used to describe nationality, profession, relationships (friend, father), and personality traits.

Examples: Soy una estadounidense. = I am an American.
Él es de Puerto Rico. = He is from Puerto Rico.
Son bomberos. = They are firefighters.
Somos amigos. = We are friends.

Escriba las oraciones en español.
Write the sentences in Spanish.

1. He is the teacher. — Él es el maestro.
2. We are friends. — Somos amigas.
3. They (the boys) are intelligent. — Ellos son inteligentes.
4. You are all from the United States. — Uds. son de los Estados Unidos.
5. I am a good student. — Soy un(a) buen(a) estudiante.

teacher = el maestro   friends = amigos/amigas   student = el estudiante
from the United States = de los Estados Unidos   intelligent = inteligente

p. 47

Más usos de "ser" / More Uses of "Ser"

Ser is used to describe a subject's personal characteristics including age, character or appearance.

Examples: Eres vieja. ....You are an old woman.
Ella es amable. ....She is nice.
Él es guapo. ....He is handsome.

Escribe las oraciones en español.

1. We are young. (joven) — Somos jóvenes.
2. He is kind. (simpático) — Él es simpático.
3. The monster is ugly. (el monstruo / feo) — El monstruo es feo.
4. The girl is pretty. (la niña / bonita) — La niña es bonita.

Ser is also used to express nationality, religion, shape, size, color and number.

Examples: Ella es de Paraguay. ....She is from Paraguay.
Él es católico. ....He is Catholic.
El árbol es verde. ....The tree is green.
Somos seis. ....We are six. (There are six of us.)

Escriba las oraciones en español.

1. She is from Mexico. — Ella es de México.
2. The boy is tall. — El niño es alto.
3. She is Hindu. — Ella es hindú.
4. His shirt is green. — Su camisa es verde.

from	=	de
tall	=	alto
Hindu	=	hindú
shirt	=	camisa

p. 48

¿Ser o estar? / "Ser" or "Estar"?

Ser is used in impersonal expressions such as "It is true" or "It is possible," in which "it" does not refer to a particular subject.

Examples: Es verdad que... ....It's true that...
Es posible que... ....It's possible that...

Ser is also used to tell time.

Examples: Es la una. ....It is one o'clock.
Son las dos. ....It is two o'clock.

Some adjectives can express either a permanent or temporary characteristic.
To describe a permanent characteristic, use ser.
To describe a temporary condition, use estar.

Examples: Él es sordo. ....He is permanently deaf.
Él está sordo. ....He is temporarily deaf (perhaps due to a cold).

Escriba la forma correcta de "estar" o "ser" para completar cada oración.

1. Mi televisión **está** estropeada. (My TV is broken.)
2. La iglesia **es** grande. (The church is big.)
3. El niño **es** inteligente. (The boy is intelligent.)
4. El niño **está** listo. (The boy is ready.)
5. Los colores **son** brillantes. (The colors are bright.)
6. **Son** las diez de la mañana. (It is 10 o'clock in the morning.)
7. La caja **está** en la esquina. (The box is in the corner.)
8. El museo **está** enfrente del parque. (The museum is across from the park.)
9. Ella **es** de España. (She is from Spain.)
10. **Es** importante estudiar. (It is important to study.)

p. 49

¿De dónde eres? / Where Are You From?

To say that you are from a particular country (or city), use ser + de + the country's name.

Conteste las preguntas en español.

Example: ¿De dónde es él? (Australia)
Él es de Australia.

1. ¿De dónde es ella? (México) — Ella es de México.
2. ¿De dónde son ustedes? (Canadá) — Somos de Canadá.
3. ¿De dónde eres? (Japón) — Soy de Japón.
4. ¿De dónde son ellos? (los Estados Unidos) — Ellos son de los Estados Unidos.
5. ¿De dónde es usted? (España) — Soy de España.
6. ¿De dónde es Ivana? (Rusia) — Ella es de Rusia.
7. ¿De dónde eres? (Chile) — Soy de Chile.
8. ¿De dónde es él? (Kenia) — Él es de Kenia.

p. 50

La comunidad / The Community

Trace una línea entre las palabras en español y las palabras en inglés.
Draw a line between the Spanish words and the English words.

la universidad	businessman
la escuela	shop
el hospital	farm
la doctora	college/university
la tienda	garage or workshop
el hombre de negocios	capital
la granja	fire station
el restaurante	waitress
el mercado	firefighter
la estación de bomberos	president
la capital	nurse
el taller	hospital
la camarera	cook
el mecánico	doctor
el presidente	mechanic
el bombero	restaurant
la enfermera	school
el cocinero	employee
la oficina	market
el empleado	office

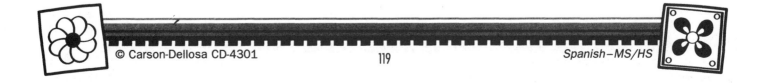

Answer Key

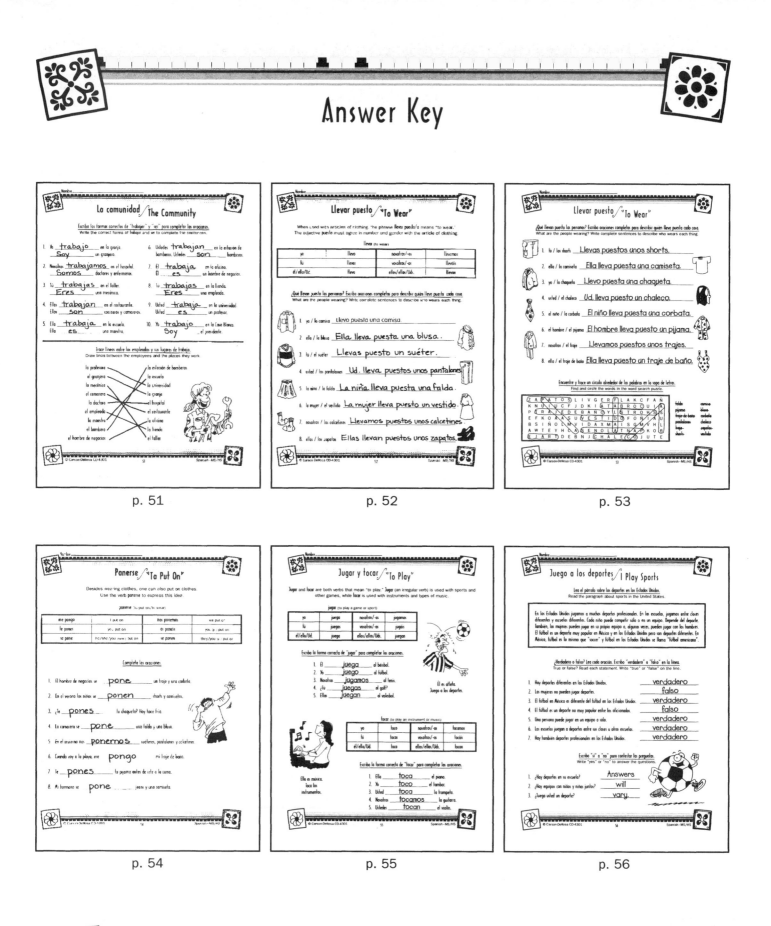

p. 51

p. 52

p. 53

p. 54

p. 55

p. 56

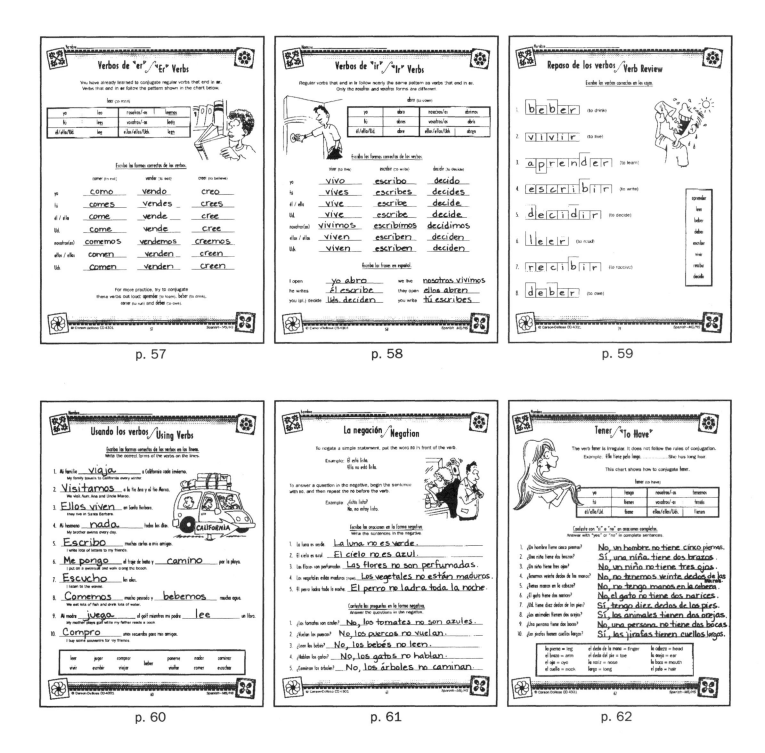

p. 57

Verbos de "er" / "Er" Verbs

You have already learned to conjugate regular verbs that end in ar.
Verbs that end in er follow the pattern shown in the chart below.

leer (to read)

yo	leo	nosotros/-as	leemos
tú	lees	vosotros/-as	leéis
él/ella/Ud.	lee	ellos/ellas/Uds.	leen

Escriba las formas correctas de los verbos.

	comer (to eat)	vender (to sell)	creer (to believe)
yo	como	vendo	creo
tú	comes	vendes	crees
él / ella	come	vende	cree
Ud.	come	vende	cree
nosotros(as)	comemos	vendemos	creemos
ellos / ellas	comen	venden	creen
Uds.	comen	venden	creen

For more practice, try to conjugate
these verbs out loud: aprender (to learn), beber (to drink),
correr (to run) and deber (to owe).

p. 58

Verbos de "ir" / "Ir" Verbs

Regular verbs that end in ir follow nearly the same pattern as verbs that end in er.
Only the nosotros and vosotros forms are different.

abrir (to open)

yo	abro	nosotros/os	abrimos
tú	abres	vosotros/os	abrís
él/ella/Ud.	abre	ellos/ellas/Uds.	abren

Escriba las formas correctas de los verbos.

	vivir (to live)	escribir (to write)	decidir (to decide)
yo	vivo	escribo	decido
tú	vives	escribes	decides
él / ella	vive	escribe	decide
Ud.	vive	escribe	decide
nosotros(as)	vivimos	escribimos	decidimos
ellos / ellas	viven	escriben	deciden
Uds.	viven	escriben	deciden

Escriba las frases en español.

I open — yo abro / we live — nosotros vivimos
he writes — él escribe / they open — ellos abren
you (pl.) decide — Uds. deciden / you write — tú escribes

p. 59

Repaso de los verbos / Verb Review

Escriba los verbos correctos en las cajas.

1. b e b e r (to drink)
2. v i v i r (to live)
3. a p r e n d e r (to learn)
4. e s c r i b i r (to write)
5. d e c i d i r (to decide)
6. l e e r (to read)
7. r e c i b i r (to receive)
8. d e b e r (to owe)

aprender
leer
beber
deber
escribir
vivir
recibir
decidir

p. 60

Usando los verbos / Using Verbs

Escriba las formas correctas de los verbos en las líneas.
Write the correct forms of the verbs on the lines.

1. Mi familia **viaja** a California cada invierno.
   My family travels to California every winter.
2. **Visitamos** a la tía Ana y al tío Marco.
   We visit Aunt Ana and Uncle Marco.
3. **Ellos viven** en Santa Bárbara.
   They live in Santa Barbara.
4. Mi hermano **nada** todos los días.
   My brother swims every day.
5. **Escribo** muchas cartas a mis amigos.
   I write lots of letters to my friends.
6. **Me pongo** el traje de baño y **camino** por la playa.
   I put on a swimsuit and walk along the beach.
7. **Escucho** las olas.
   I listen to the waves.
8. **Comemos** mucho pescado y **bebemos** mucha agua.
   We eat lots of fish and drink lots of water.
9. Mi madre **juega** al golf mientras mi padre **lee** un libro.
   My mother plays golf while my father reads a book.
10. **Compro** unos recuerdos para mis amigos.
    I buy some souvenirs for my friends.

leer, jugar, comprar, beber, ponerse, nadar, caminar
vivir, escribir, viajar, visitar, comer, escuchar

p. 61

La negación / Negation

To negate a simple statement, put the word no in front of the verb.
Example: Él está listo.
Él no está listo.

To answer a question in the negative, begin the sentence
with no, and then repeat the no before the verb.
Example: ¿Estás listo?
No, no estoy listo.

Escriba las oraciones en la forma negativa.
Write the sentences in the negative.

1. La luna es verde. **La luna no es verde.**
2. El cielo es azul. **El cielo no es azul.**
3. Las flores son perfumadas. **Las flores no son perfumadas.**
4. Los vegetales están maduros (ripe). **Los vegetales no están maduros.**
5. El perro ladra toda la noche. **El perro no ladra toda la noche.**

Conteste las preguntas en la forma negativa.
Answer the questions in the negative.

1. ¿Los tomates son azules? **No, los tomates no son azules.**
2. ¿Vuelan los puercos? **No, los puercos no vuelan.**
3. ¿Leen los bebés? **No, los bebés no leen.**
4. ¿Hablan los gatos? **No, los gatos no hablan.**
5. ¿Caminan los árboles? **No, los árboles no caminan.**

p. 62

Tener / "To Have"

The verb tener is irregular. It does not follow the rules of conjugation.
Example: Ella tiene pelo largo. .... She has long hair.

This chart shows how to conjugate tener.

tener (to have)

yo	tengo	nosotros/-as	tenemos
tú	tienes	vosotros/-as	tenéis
él/ella/Ud.	tiene	ellos/ellas/Uds.	tienen

Conteste con "sí" o "no" en oraciones completas.
Answer with "yes" or "no" in complete sentences.

1. ¿Un hombre tiene cinco piernas? **No, un hombre no tiene cinco piernas.**
2. ¿Una niña tiene dos brazos? **Sí, una niña tiene dos brazos.**
3. ¿Un niño tiene tres ojos? **No, un niño no tiene tres ojos.**
4. ¿Tenemos veinte dedos de las manos? **No, no tenemos veinte dedos de las manos.**
5. ¿Tienes manos en la cabeza? **No, no tengo manos en la cabeza.**
6. ¿El gato tiene dos narices? **No, el gato no tiene dos narices.**
7. ¿Ud. tiene diez dedos de los pies? **Sí, tengo diez dedos de los pies.**
8. ¿Los animales tienen dos orejas? **Sí, los animales tienen dos orejas.**
9. ¿Una persona tiene dos bocas? **No, una persona no tiene dos bocas.**
10. ¿Las jirafas tienen cuellos largos? **Sí, las jirafas tienen cuellos largos.**

la pierna = leg	el dedo de la mano = finger	la cabeza = head
el brazo = arm	el dedo del pie = toe	la oreja = ear
el ojo = eye	la nariz = nose	la boca = mouth
el cuello = neck	largo = long	el pelo = hair

Answer Key

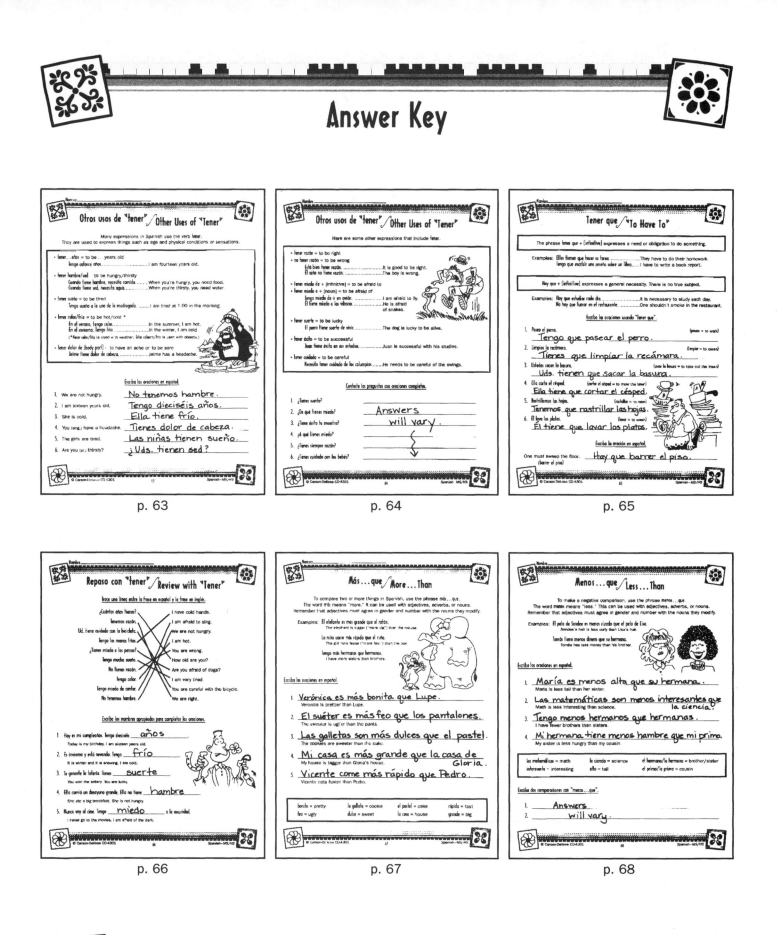

p. 63

p. 64

p. 65

p. 66

p. 67

p. 68

Answer Key

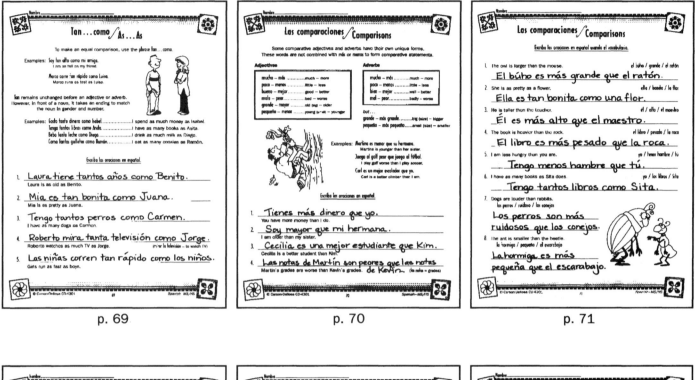

p. 69   p. 70   p. 71

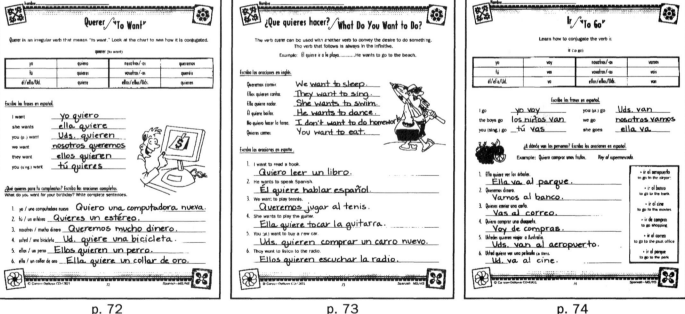

p. 72   p. 73   p. 74

Answer Key

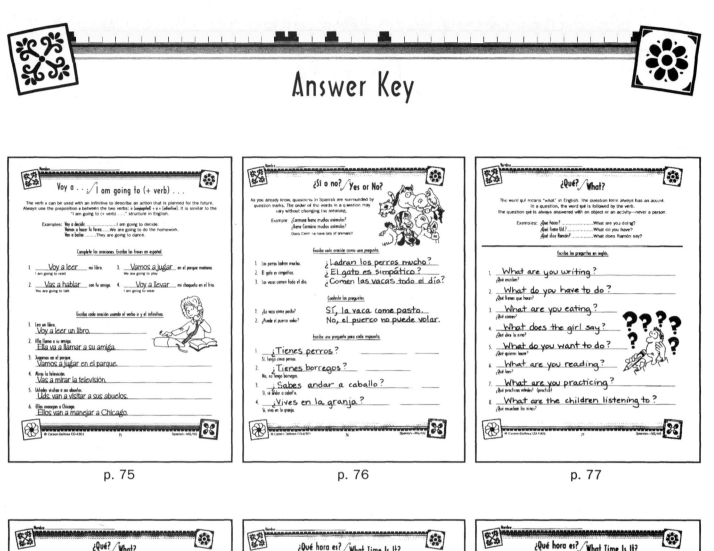

p. 75

Voy a . . . / I am going to (+ verb) . . .

The verb *ir* can be used with an infinitive to describe an action that is planned for the future. Always use the preposition *a* between the two verbs: ir (conjugated) + *a* + (infinitive). It is similar to the "I am going to (+ verb) . . ." structure in English.

Examples: Voy a decidir. . . . . .I am going to decide.
Vamos a hacer la tarea. . . . . .We are going to do the homework.
Van a bailar. . . . . .They are going to dance.

Complete las oraciones. Escriba las frases en español.

1. **Voy a leer** mi libro.
   (I am going to read)
2. **Vas a hablar** con tu amigo.
   (You are going to talk)
3. **Vamos a jugar** en el parque mañana.
   (We are going to play)
4. **Voy a llevar** mi chaqueta en el frío.
   (I am going to wear)

Escriba cada oración usando el verbo ir y el infinitivo.

1. Leo un libro.
   Voy a leer un libro.
2. Ella llama a su amiga.
   Ella va a llamar a su amiga.
3. Jugamos en el parque.
   Vamos a jugar en el parque.
4. Miras la televisión.
   Vas a mirar la televisión.
5. Ustedes visitan a sus abuelos.
   Uds. van a visitar a sus abuelos.
6. Ellos manejan a Chicago.
   Ellos van a manejar a Chicago.

p. 76

¿Sí o no? / Yes or No?

As you already know, questions in Spanish are surrounded by question marks. The order of the words in a question may vary without changing the meaning.

Example: ¿Carmina tiene muchos animales?
¿Tiene Carmina muchos animales?
Does Carmina have lots of animals?

Escriba cada oración como una pregunta.

1. Los perros ladran mucho.
   ¿Ladran los perros mucho?
2. El gato es simpático.
   ¿El gato es simpático?
3. Las vacas comen todo el día.
   ¿Comen las vacas todo el día?

Conteste las preguntas.

1. ¿La vaca come pasto?
   Sí, la vaca come pasto.
2. ¿Puede el puerco volar?
   No, el puerco no puede volar.

Escriba una pregunta para cada respuesta.

1. **¿Tienes perros?**
   Sí, tengo cinco perros.
2. **¿Tienes borregos?**
   No, no tengo borregos.
3. **¿Sabes andar a caballo?**
   Sí, se andar a caballo.
4. **¿Vives en la granja?**
   Sí, vivo en la granja.

p. 77

¿Qué? / What?

The word *qué* means "what" in English. The question form always has an accent. In a question, the word *qué* is followed by the verb. The question *qué* is always answered with an object or an activity—never a person.

Examples: ¿Qué haces? . . . . .What are you doing?
¿Qué tiene Ud.? . . . . .What do you have?
¿Qué dice Ramón? . . . . .What does Ramón say?

Escriba las preguntas en inglés.

1. **What are you writing?**
   ¿Qué escribes?
2. **What do you have to do?**
   ¿Qué tienes que hacer?
3. **What are you eating?**
   ¿Qué comes?
4. **What does the girl say?**
   ¿Qué dice la niña?
5. **What do you want to do?**
   ¿Qué quieres hacer?
6. **What are you reading?**
   ¿Qué lees?
7. **What are you practicing?**
   ¿Qué practican ustedes? (practice)
8. **What are the children listening to?**
   ¿Qué escuchan los niños?

p. 78

¿Qué? / What?

Escriba la pregunta apropiada usando "qué".

1. Tengo un vestido nuevo. — **¿Qué tienes?**
2. Escuchamos la música de Brasil. — **¿Qué escuchan Uds.?**
3. Juegan con sus amigos esta tarde. — **¿Qué hacen ellos esta tarde?**
4. La lección es la de la página dos. — **¿Qué es la lección?**
5. Son mis libros. — **¿Qué son?**
6. Como una hamburguesa. — **¿Qué comes?**
7. Él lee una revista. — **¿Qué lee él?**
8. Miramos los dibujos animados (cartoons). — **¿Qué miran Uds.?**
9. La niña pinta un dibujo de los árboles. — **¿Qué pinta la niña?**
10. Ella hace galletas. — **¿Qué hace ella?**

Trace una línea entre la pregunta y la respuesta apropiada.

¿Qué comen los niños? — Yo leo un libro.
¿Qué llevas? — Nosotros escribimos una carta.
¿Qué lees? — Está nevando.
¿Qué escriben? — Ellos comen unas fresas.
¿Qué tiempo hace? — Llevo un suéter nuevo.

p. 79

¿Qué hora es? / What Time Is It?

To ask what time it is in Spanish, say ¿Qué hora es?
To answer, say Son las and the number of the hour.
One o'clock is expressed: Es la una.

Examples: ¿Qué hora es? . . . . .What time is it?
Es la una. . . . . .It is one o'clock.
Son las dos. . . . . .It is two o'clock.

Add minutes to the current hour up to 30 minutes. Use the word *y*.
After 30, subtract the minutes from the next hour. Use the word *menos*.

Examples: Son las seis y diez. . . . .It is 6:10.
Son las tres menos diez. . . . .It is 2:50. (three minus ten)

Escriba las horas.

Es la una. **1:00**
Son las tres y veinte. **3:20**
Son las cinco y quince. **5:15**
Son las nueve menos diez. **8:50**
Son las ocho menos veinticinco. **7:35**
Son la una y treinta y cinco. **1:35**

Escriba las horas en español.

Son las tres.
Son las ocho menos cinco.
4:05 **Son las cuatro y cinco.**
2:35 **Son las tres menos veinticinco.**
6:10 **Son las seis y diez.**
1:25 **Es la una y veinticinco.**
3:40 **Son las cuatro menos veinte.**

p. 80

¿Qué hora es? / What Time Is It?

Here are some other common time expressions.

10:00	Son las diez en punto (on the dot).
12:15	Son las doce y cuarto (quarter).
7:30	Son las siete y media (half).
5:45	Son las seis menos cuarto.

Escriba las horas.

Es la una y media. **1:30**
Son las once y cuarto. **11:15**
Son las nueve menos cuarto. **8:45**
Son las cuatro en punto. **4:00**

de la madrugada = in the morning (very early)
de la mañana = in the morning
de la tarde = in the afternoon
de la noche = in the evening / at night

Escriba las horas en español.

4:15 **Son las cuatro y cuarto.**
2:30 **Son las dos y media.**
6:08 **Son las seis y ocho.**
1:23 A.M. **Es la una y veintitrés de la madrugada.**
4:45 P.M. **Son las cinco menos cuarto de la tarde.**

Trace una línea entre la hora y la frase correcta en español.

3:00 — Es la una menos cuarto.
1:15 — Son las tres y media.
12:45 — Son las doce y cuarto.
3:30 — Son las tres en punto.
12:15 — Es la una y cuarto.

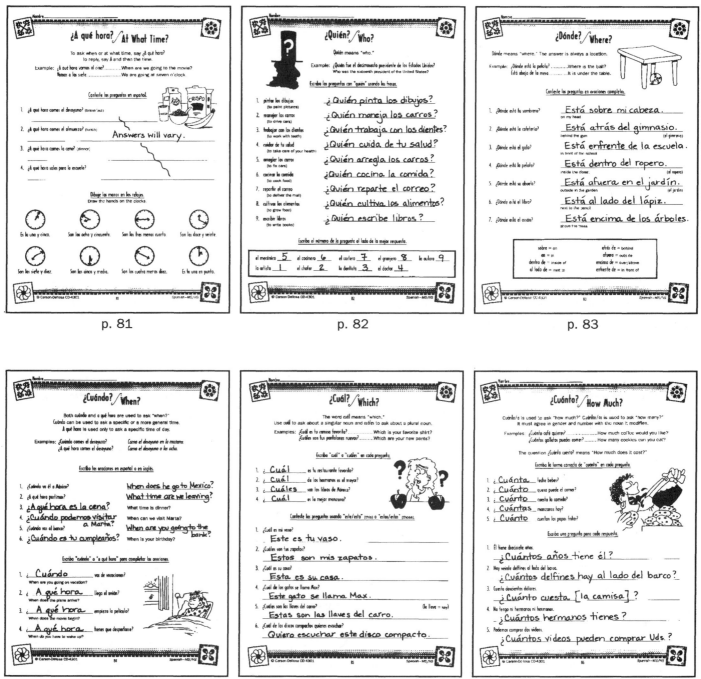

p. 81 — ¿A qué hora? / At What Time?

To ask when or at what time, say ¿A qué hora?
To reply, say a and then the time.

Example: ¿A qué hora vamos al cine? .... When are we going to the movie?
Vamos a las siete. .... We are going at seven o'clock.

Conteste las preguntas en español.

1. ¿A qué hora comes el desayuno? (breakfast)

2. ¿A qué hora comes el almuerzo? (lunch)

3. ¿A qué hora comes la cena? (dinner)

4. ¿A qué hora sales para la escuela?

Answers will vary.

Dibuje las manos en los relojes.
Draw the hands on the clocks.

Es la una y cinco. Son las ocho y cincuenta. Son las tres menos cuarto. Son las doce y veinte.
Son las siete y diez. Son las cinco y media. Son las cuatro menos diez. Es la una en punto.

p. 82 — ¿Quién? / Who?

Quién means "who."

Example: ¿Quién fue el décimosexto presidente de los Estados Unidos?
Who was the sixteenth president of the United States?

Escriba las preguntas con "quién" usando las frases.

1. pintar los dibujos (to paint pictures) — ¿Quién pinta los dibujos?
2. manejar los carros (to drive cars) — ¿Quién maneja los carros?
3. trabajar con los dientes (to work with teeth) — ¿Quién trabaja con los dientes?
4. cuidar de tu salud (to take care of your health) — ¿Quién cuida de tu salud?
5. arreglar los carros (to fix cars) — ¿Quién arregla los carros?
6. cocinar la comida (to cook food) — ¿Quién cocina la comida?
7. repartir el correo (to deliver the mail) — ¿Quién reparte el correo?
8. cultivar los alimentos (to grow food) — ¿Quién cultiva los alimentos?
9. escribir libros (to write books) — ¿Quién escribe libros?

Escriba el número de la pregunta al lado de la mejor respuesta.

el mecánico 5   el cocinero 6   el cartero 7   el granjero 8   la autora 9
la artista 1   el chofer 2   la dentista 3   el doctor 4

p. 83 — ¿Dónde? / Where?

Dónde means "where." The answer is always a location.

Example: ¿Dónde está la pelota? .... Where is the ball?
Está abajo de la mesa. .... It is under the table.

Conteste las preguntas en oraciones completas.

1. ¿Dónde está tu sombrero? — Está sobre mi cabeza. (on my head)
2. ¿Dónde está la cafetería? — Está atrás del gimnasio. (behind the gym) (el gimnasio)
3. ¿Dónde está el gato? — Está enfrente de la escuela. (in front of the school)
4. ¿Dónde está la pelota? — Está dentro del ropero. (inside the closet) (el ropero)
5. ¿Dónde está su abuela? — Está afuera en el jardín. (outside in the garden) (el jardín)
6. ¿Dónde está el libro? — Está al lado del lápiz. (next to the pencil)
7. ¿Dónde está el avión? — Está encima de los árboles. (above the trees)

sobre = on
en = in
dentro de = inside of
al lado de = next to
atrás de = behind
afuera = outside
encima de = over/above
enfrente de = in front of

p. 84 — ¿Cuándo? / When?

Both cuándo and a qué hora are used to ask "when?"
Cuándo can be used to ask a specific or a more general time.
A qué hora is used only to ask a specific time of day.

Examples: ¿Cuándo comes el desayuno? Como el desayuno en la mañana.
¿A qué hora comes el desayuno? Como el desayuno a las ocho.

Escriba las oraciones en español o en inglés.

1. ¿Cuándo va él a México? — When does he go to Mexico?
2. ¿A qué hora partimos? — What time are we leaving?
3. ¿A qué hora es la cena? — What time is dinner?
4. ¿Cuándo podemos visitar a Marta? — When can we visit Marta?
5. ¿Cuándo vas al banco? — When are you going to the bank?
6. ¿Cuándo es tu cumpleaños? — When is your birthday?

Escriba "cuándo" o "a qué hora" para completar las oraciones.

1. ¿Cuándo vas de vacaciones? (When are you going on vacation?)
2. ¿A qué hora llega el avión? (When does the plane arrive?)
3. ¿A qué hora empieza la película? (When does the movie begin?)
4. ¿A qué hora tienes que despertarte? (When do you have to wake up?)

p. 85 — ¿Cuál? / Which?

The word cuál means "which."
Use cuál to ask about a singular noun and cuáles to ask about a plural noun.

Examples: ¿Cuál es tu camisa favorita? Which is your favorite shirt?
¿Cuáles son tus pantalones nuevos? Which are your new pants?

Escriba "cuál" o "cuáles" en cada pregunta.

1. ¿Cuál es tu restaurante favorito?
2. ¿Cuál de los hermanos es el mayor?
3. ¿Cuáles son los libros de Mónica?
4. ¿Cuál es la mejor manzana?

Conteste las preguntas usando "este/esta" (this) o "estos/estas" (those).

1. ¿Cuál es mi vaso? — Este es tu vaso.
2. ¿Cuáles son tus zapatos? — Estos son mis zapatos.
3. ¿Cuál es su casa? — Esta es su casa.
4. ¿Cuál de los gatos se llama Max? — Este gato se llama Max.
5. ¿Cuáles son las llaves del carro? (la llave = key) — Estas son las llaves del carro.
6. ¿Cuál de los discos compactos quieres escuchar? — Quiero escuchar este disco compacto.

p. 86 — ¿Cuánto? / How Much?

Cuánto/a/s is used to ask "how much?" Cuántos/as is used to ask "how many?"
It must agree in gender and number with the noun it modifies.

Examples: ¿Cuánto café quieres? .... How much coffee would you like?
¿Cuántas galletas puedes comer? .... How many cookies can you eat?

The question ¿Cuánto cuesta? means "How much does it cost?"

Escriba la forma correcta de "cuánto" en cada pregunta.

1. ¿Cuánta leche bebes?
2. ¿Cuánto queso puede él comer?
3. ¿Cuánto cuesta la comida?
4. ¿Cuántas manzanas hay?
5. ¿Cuánto cuestan los papas fritas?

Escriba una pregunta para cada respuesta.

1. Él tiene diecisiete años. — ¿Cuántos años tiene él?
2. Hay veinte delfines al lado del barco. — ¿Cuántos delfines hay al lado del barco?
3. Cuesta doscientos dólares. — ¿Cuánto cuesta [la camisa]?
4. No tengo ni hermanos ni hermanas. — ¿Cuántos hermanos tienes?
5. Podemos comprar dos videos. — ¿Cuántos videos pueden comprar Uds.?

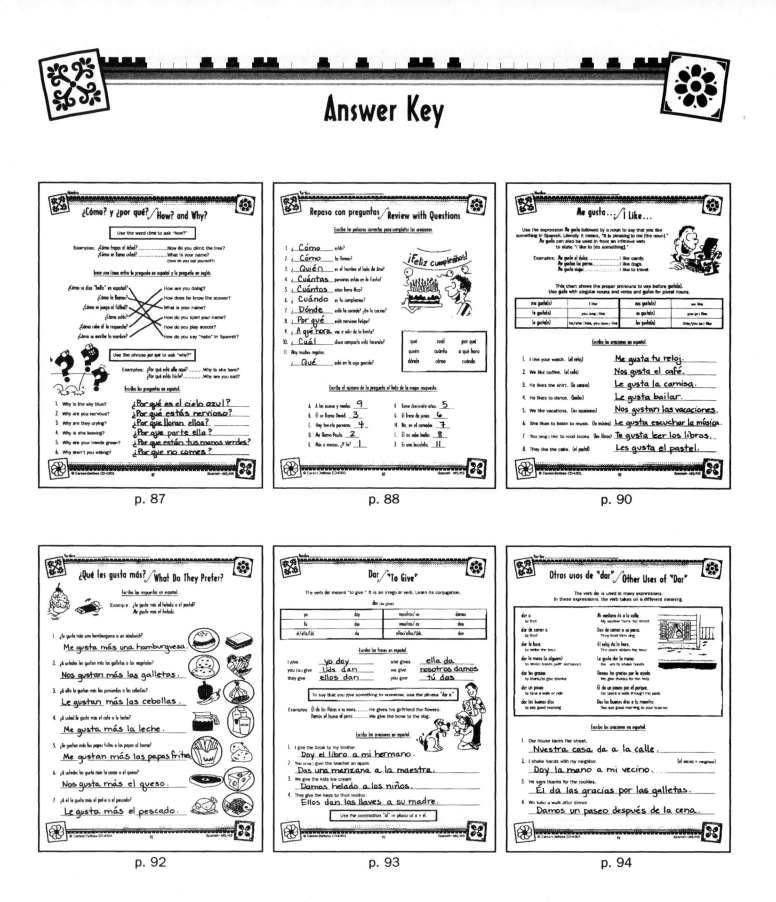

p. 87 — ¿Cómo? y ¿por qué? / How? and Why?

Use the word *cómo* to ask "how?"

Examples: ¿Cómo trepas el árbol? ....How do you climb the tree?
¿Cómo se llama usted? ....What is your name? (How do you call yourself?)

Trace una línea entre la pregunta en español y la pregunta en inglés.

¿Cómo se dice "hello" en español? — How are you doing?
¿Cómo te llamas? — How does he know the answer?
¿Cómo se juega al fútbol? — What is your name?
¿Cómo estás? — How do you spell your name?
¿Cómo sabe él la respuesta? — How do you play soccer?
¿Cómo se escribe tu nombre? — How do you say "hello" in Spanish?

Use the phrase *por qué* to ask "why?"

Examples: ¿Por qué está ella aquí? ....Why is she here?
¿Por qué está triste? ....Why are you sad?

Escribe las preguntas en español.

1. Why is the sky blue? — ¿Por qué es el cielo azul?
2. Why are you nervous? — ¿Por qué estás nervioso?
3. Why are they crying? — ¿Por qué lloran ellos?
4. Why is she leaving? — ¿Por qué parte ella?
5. Why are your hands green? — ¿Por qué están tus manos verdes?
6. Why aren't you eating? — ¿Por qué no comes?

p. 88 — Repaso con preguntas / Review with Questions

Escribe las palabras correctas para completar las oraciones.

1. ¿Cómo estás?
2. ¿Cómo te llamas?
3. ¿Quién es el hombre al lado de Ana?
4. ¿Cuántas personas están en la fiesta?
5. ¿Cuántos años tiene Nico?
6. ¿Cuándo es tu cumpleaños?
7. ¿Dónde está la comida? ¿En la cocina?
8. ¿Por qué está nervioso Felipe?
9. ¿A qué hora vas a salir de la fiesta?
10. ¿Cuál disco compacto está tocando?
11. Hay muchos regalos. ¿Qué está en la caja grande?

¡Feliz cumpleaños!

qué	cuál	por qué
quién	cuándo	a qué hora
dónde	cómo	cuándo

Escribe el número de la pregunta al lado de la mejor respuesta.

A. A las nueve y media. — 9
B. Él se llama David. — 3
C. Hay treinta personas. — 4
D. Me llamo Paula. — 2
E. Más o menos. ¿Y tú? — 1
F. Tiene dieciséis años. — 5
G. El trece de junio. — 6
H. No, en el comedor. — 7
I. Él no sabe bailar. — 8
J. Es una bicicleta. — 11

p. 90 — Me gusta... / I Like...

Use the expression *Me gusta* followed by a noun to say that you like something in Spanish. Literally, it means, "It is pleasing to me (the noun)." *Me gusta* can also be used in front of an infinitive verb to state "I like to (do something)."

Examples: Me gusta el dulce. ....I like candy.
Me gustan los perros. ....I like dogs.
Me gusta viajar. ....I like to travel.

This chart shows the proper pronouns to use before *gusta(n)*. Use *gusta* with singular nouns and verbs and *gustan* for plural nouns.

me gusta(n)	I like	nos gusta(n)	we like
te gusta(n)	you (sing.) like	os gusta(n)	you (pl.) like
le gusta(n)	he/she likes, you (form.) like	les gusta(n)	they/you (pl.) like

Escribe las oraciones en español.

1. I like your watch. (el reloj) — Me gusta tu reloj.
2. We like coffee. (el café) — Nos gusta el café.
3. He likes the shirt. (la camisa) — Le gusta la camisa.
4. He likes to dance. (bailar) — Le gusta bailar.
5. We like vacations. (las vacaciones) — Nos gustan las vacaciones.
6. She likes to listen to music. (la música) — Le gusta escuchar la música.
7. You (sing.) like to read books. (los libros) — Te gusta leer los libros.
8. They like the cake. (el pastel) — Les gusta el pastel.

p. 92 — ¿Qué les gusta más? / What Do They Prefer?

Escribe las respuestas en español.

Ejemplo: ¿Le gusta más el helado o el pastel?
Me gusta más el helado.

1. ¿Te gusta más una hamburguesa o un sándwich?
Me gusta más una hamburguesa.
2. ¿A ustedes les gustan más las galletas o los vegetales?
Nos gustan más las galletas.
3. ¿A ella le gustan más los pimientos o las cebollas?
Le gustan más las cebollas.
4. ¿A usted le gusta más el café o la leche?
Me gusta más la leche.
5. ¿Te gustan más las papas fritas o las papas al horno?
Me gustan más las papas fritas.
6. ¿A ustedes les gusta más la carne o el queso?
Nos gusta más el queso.
7. ¿A él le gusta más el pollo o el pescado?
Le gusta más el pescado.

p. 93 — Dar / "To Give"

The verb *dar* means "to give." It is an irregular verb. Learn its conjugation.

dar (to give)

yo	doy	nosotros/-as	damos
tú	das	vosotros/-as	dais
él/ella/Ud.	da	ellos/ellas/Uds.	dan

Escribe las frases en español.

I give	yo doy	she gives	ella da
you (s.) give	Uds. dan	we give	nosotros damos
they give	ellos dan	you give	tú das

To say that you give something to someone, use the phrase *dar a.*

Examples: Él da las flores a su novia. ....He gives his girlfriend the flowers.
Damos el hueso al perro. ....We give the bone to the dog.

Escribe las oraciones en español.

1. I give the book to my brother.
Doy el libro a mi hermano.
2. You (sing.) give the teacher an apple.
Das una manzana a la maestra.
3. We give the kids ice cream.
Damos helado a los niños.
4. They give the keys to their mother.
Ellos dan las llaves a su madre.

Use the contraction "al" in place of a + el.

p. 94 — Otros usos de "dar" / Other Uses of "Dar"

The verb *dar* is used in many expressions. In these expressions, the verb takes on a different meaning.

dar a — to face	Mi ventana da a la calle. — My window faces the street.
dar de comer a — to feed	Dan de comer a su perro. — They feed their dog.
dar la hora — to strike the hour	El reloj da la hora. — The clock strikes the hour.
dar la mano a (alguien) — to shake hands (with someone)	Le gusta dar la mano. — He likes to shake hands.
dar las gracias — to thank/to give thanks	Damos las gracias por la ayuda. — We give thanks for the help.
dar un paseo — to take a walk or ride	Él da un paseo por el parque. — He takes a walk through the park.
dar los buenos días — to say good morning	Das los buenos días a tu maestra. — You say good morning to your teacher.

Escribe las oraciones en español.

1. Our house faces the street.
Nuestra casa da a la calle.
2. I shake hands with my neighbor. (el vecino = neighbor)
Doy la mano a mi vecino.
3. He says thanks for the cookies.
Él da las gracias por las galletas.
4. We take a walk after dinner.
Damos un paseo después de la cena.

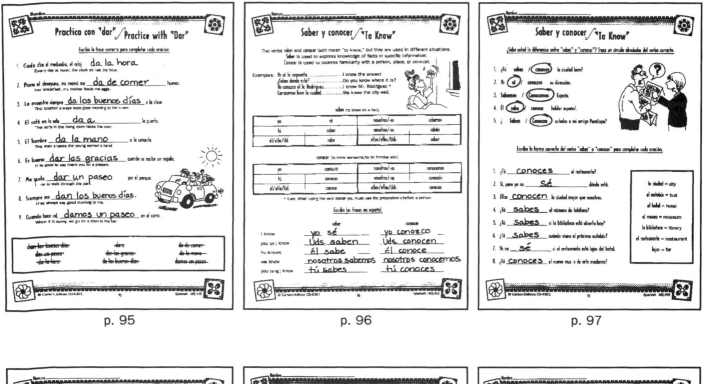

p. 95

p. 96

p. 97

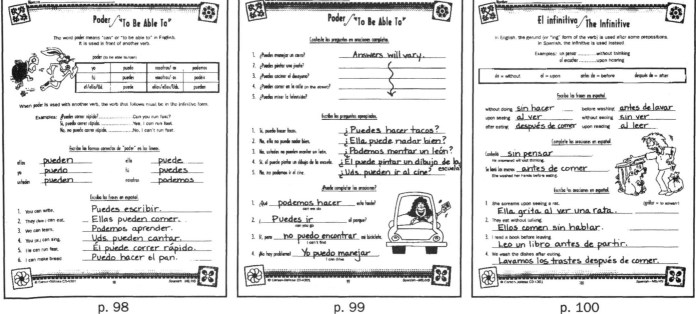

p. 98

p. 99

p. 100

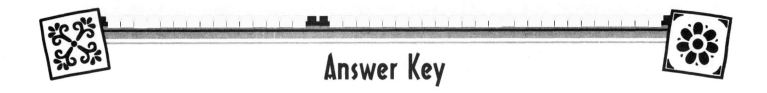

Answer Key

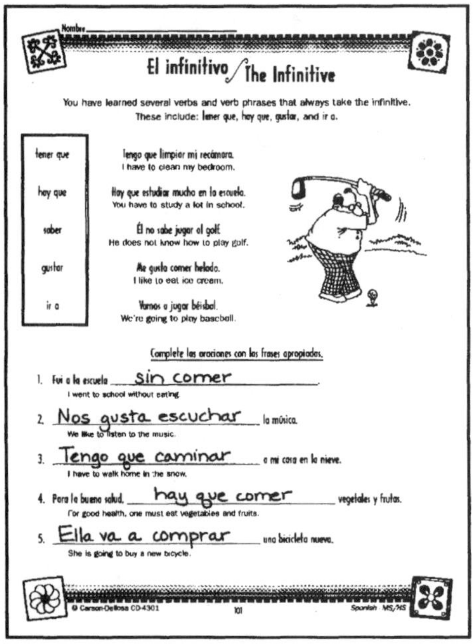
Nombre
El infinitivo / The Infinitive
You have learned several verbs and verb phrases that always take the infinitive. These include: tener que, hay que, gustar, and ir a.
tener que — Tengo que limpiar mi recámara. I have to clean my bedroom.
hay que — Hay que estudiar mucho en la escuela. You have to study a lot in school.
saber — Él no sabe jugar al golf. He does not know how to play golf.
gustar — Me gusta comer helado. I like to eat ice cream.
ir a — Vamos a jugar béisbol. We're going to play baseball.
Complete las oraciones con las frases apropiadas.
1. Fui a la escuela sin comer. I went to school without eating.
2. Nos gusta escuchar la música. We like to listen to the music.
3. Tengo que caminar a mi casa en la nieve. I have to walk home in the snow.
4. Para la buena salud, hay que comer vegetales y frutas. For good health, one must eat vegetables and fruits.
5. Ella va a comprar una bicicleta nueva. She is going to buy a new bicycle.
© Carson-Dellosa CD-4301 101 Spanish–MS/HS

p. 101

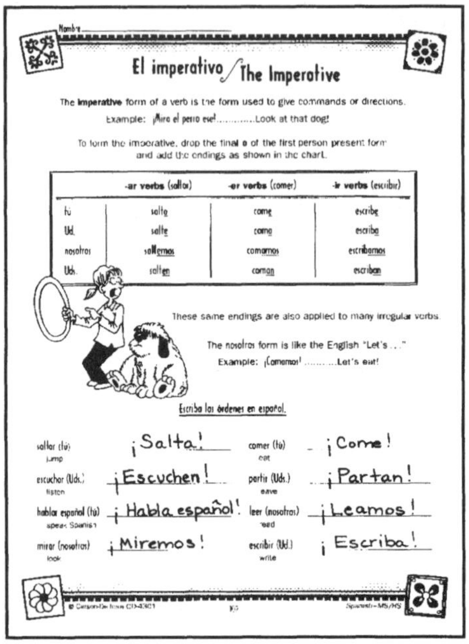
Nombre
El imperativo / The Imperative
The imperative form of a verb is the form used to give commands or directions.
Example: ¡Mira el perro ese! ....Look at that dog!
To form the imperative, drop the final o of the first person present form and add the endings as shown in the chart.
-ar verbs (saltar) | -er verbs (comer) | -ir verbs (escribir)
tú: salta | come | escribe
Ud.: salte | coma | escriba
nosotros: saltemos | comamos | escribamos
Uds.: salten | coman | escriban
These same endings are also applied to many irregular verbs.
The nosotros form is like the English "Let's . . ."
Example: ¡Comamos! ....Let's eat!
Escriba las órdenes en español.
saltar (tú) jump — ¡Salta!
comer (tú) eat — ¡Come!
escuchar (Uds.) listen — ¡Escuchen!
partir (Uds.) leave — ¡Partan!
hablar español (tú) speak Spanish — ¡Habla español!
leer (nosotros) read — ¡Leamos!
mirar (nosotros) look — ¡Miremos!
escribir (Ud.) write — ¡Escriba!
© Carson-Dellosa CD-4301 102 Spanish–MS/HS

p. 102

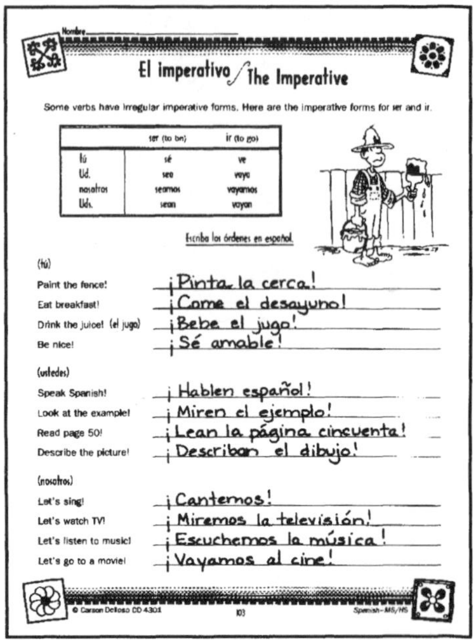
Nombre
El imperativo / The Imperative
Some verbs have irregular imperative forms. Here are the imperative forms for ser and ir.
ser (to be) | ir (to go)
tú: sé | ve
Ud.: sea | vaya
nosotros: seamos | vayamos
Uds.: sean | vayan
Escriba las órdenes en español.
(tú)
Paint the fence! ¡Pinta la cerca!
Eat breakfast! ¡Come el desayuno!
Drink the juice! (el jugo) ¡Bebe el jugo!
Be nice! ¡Sé amable!
(ustedes)
Speak Spanish! ¡Hablen español!
Look at the example! ¡Miren el ejemplo!
Read page 50! ¡Lean la página cincuenta!
Describe the picture! ¡Describan el dibujo!
(nosotros)
Let's sing! ¡Cantemos!
Let's watch TV! ¡Miremos la televisión!
Let's listen to music! ¡Escuchemos la música!
Let's go to a movie! ¡Vayamos al cine!
© Carson-Dellosa CD-4301 103 Spanish–MS/HS

p. 103

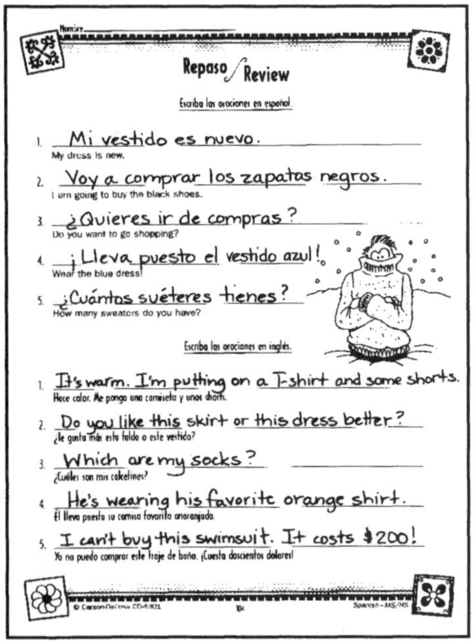
Nombre
Repaso / Review
Escriba las oraciones en español.
1. Mi vestido es nuevo. My dress is new.
2. Voy a comprar los zapatos negros. I am going to buy the black shoes.
3. ¿Quieres ir de compras? Do you want to go shopping?
4. ¡Lleva puesto el vestido azul! Wear the blue dress!
5. ¿Cuántos suéteres tienes? How many sweaters do you have?
Escriba las oraciones en inglés.
1. It's warm. I'm putting on a T-shirt and some shorts. Hace calor. Me pongo una camiseta y unos shorts.
2. Do you like this skirt or this dress better? ¿Le gusta más esta falda o este vestido?
3. Which are my socks? ¿Cuáles son mis calcetines?
4. He's wearing his favorite orange shirt. Él lleva puesta su camisa favorita anaranjada.
5. I can't buy this swimsuit. It costs $200! Yo no puedo comprar este traje de baño. ¡Cuesta doscientos dolares!
© Carson-Dellosa CD-4301 104 Spanish–MS/HS

p. 104

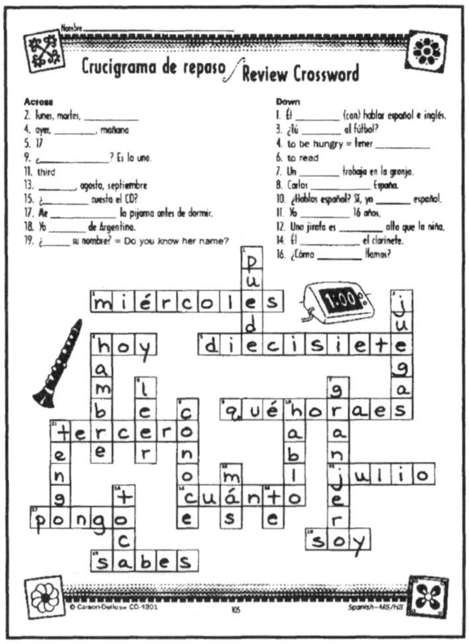
Nombre
Crucigrama de repaso / Review Crossword
Across
2. lunes, martes, ______
4. ayer, ______, mañana
5. 17
9. ¿______? Es la una.
11. third
13. ______, agosto, septiembre
15. ¿______ cuesta el CD?
17. Me ______ la pijama antes de dormir.
18. Yo ______ de Argentina.
19. ¿______ su nombre? = Do you know her name?
Down
1. Él ______ (can) hablar español e inglés.
3. ¿Tú ______ al fútbol?
4. to be hungry = tener ______
6. to read
7. Un ______ trabaja en la granja.
8. Carlos ______ España.
10. ¿Hablas español? Sí, yo ______ español.
11. Yo ______ 16 años.
12. Una jirafa es ______ alta que la niña.
14. Él ______ el clarinete.
16. ¿Cómo ______ llamas?
miércoles
hoy
diecisiete
qué hora es
tercero
julio
cuánto
pongo
soy
sabes
1:00
© Carson-Dellosa CD-4301 105 Spanish–MS/HS

p. 105